THE SCENT OF ROSES

ZINNIE HARRIS

D1375375

The Scent of Roses was first performed
at the Royal Lyceum Theatre Edinburgh on 25 February 2022

THE SCENT OF ROSES

By Zinnie Harris

Cast

in alphabetical order

Saskia Ashdown	Sally
Maureen Beattie	Helen
Leah Byrne	Caitlin
Peter Forbes	Christopher
Neve McIntosh	Luci

Creative Team

Writer and Director	**Zinnie Harris**
Designer	**Tom Piper**
Composer and Sound Designer	**Niroshini Thambar**
Lighting Designer	**Ben Ormerod**
Movement Directors	**White & Givan**
Fight Director	**Kaitlin Howard**
Intimacy Director	**Vanessa Coffey**
Casting Directors	**Simone Pereira Hind CDG and Anna Dawson**

Company Stage Manager	**Owen Thomas**
Deputy Stage Manager	**Claire Williamson**
Assistant Stage Manager	**Jessica Ward**
Script Associate	**Jackie Crichton**
Costume Supervisor	**Morag Pirrie**
Dressers	**Cleo Rose McCabe**
	Ola Szczygiel
Set Builders	**Splinter Scenery**

Credits

The Scent of Roses was made at the Royal Lyceum Theatre Edinburgh.

Zinnie Harris wishes to thank Vicky Featherstone, Berwin Lee, the Royal Court Theatre, Mark and Francesca Shaw, Emily Ingram, Morven Macbeth, Andy Clark, Charlie Oscar, Jamie Marie Leary and Fletcher Mathers.

The Scent of Roses is the recipient of a Berwin Lee New Play Commission and was made with the support of Brenda Rennie.

The Lyceum's 2021/22 Season productions were developed with support from the Stephen W Dunn Theatre Fund.

CAST

SASKIA ASHDOWN | Sally

Theatre credits for the Royal Lyceum Theatre Edinburgh include: *Lament for Sheku Bayoh* (a co-production with National Theatre of Scotland and Edinburgh International Festival); *An Edinburgh Christmas Carol*, *Who Are You?* and *History* (Sound Stage – Lyceum Theatre/Pitlochry Festival Theatre).

Other theatre credits include: *Ghost Stories* (Pitlochry Festival Theatre); *Jack Absolute Flies Again* (National Theatre); *Horizontal Collaboration* (Fire Exit).

Film, Television and Audio Drama credits include: *The Last Bus* (Hurricane Films); *Falling for Figaro* (Black Camel Pictures); *Special Delivery* (Shudder Films); *Annika* (Black Camel Pictures); *Casualty* (BBC); *Trust Me* (Red Productions); *Clique* (BBC); *Earwig* (Tron Theatre).

MAUREEN BEATTIE | Helen

Theatre credits for the Royal Lyceum Theatre Edinburgh: *Tennis Elbow* and *Helping Hands* (Sound Stage – Lyceum Theatre/Pitlochry Festival Theatre); *The Cherry Orchard*, *The Winter's Tale*.

Other theatre credits include: *The Histories* (RSC); *Othello* (National Theatre of Great Britain); *Meet Jan Black* (Gaiety, Ayr); *Go On* (Citizens Theatre at The Tron); *As You Like It* (Regent's Park Open Air Theatre); *Death of a Salesman* (Manchester Royal Exchange); *Yerma* (Young Vic/Park Avenue Armory New York); *Nuclear War*, *No Quarter* (Royal Court Theatre); *The Ferryman* (Gielguld Theatre, West End); *Right Now* (Ustinov/Bush/Traverse); *John Gabriel Barclay* (Òran Mór); *Romeo and Juliet* (Rose Theatre Kingston); *The Jennifer Tremblay Trilogy* (Edinburgh Fringe/tour); *Yer Granny* (tour); *Noises Off* (Old Vic and Tour); *Medea* (Fruitmarket, Edinburgh Fringe, tour).

Film, Television and Audio Drama credits include: *Spores* (Hopscotch Films); *Decoy Bride* (Decoy Productions); *Deadwater Fell* (Kudos for Channel 4); *Outlander* (Starz); *Doctor Who Christmas Special* (BBC); *Casualty* (BBC); *Midsomer Murders* (ITV); *Vera* (ITV); *Lewis* (Granada); *The Bill* (Thames Television); *The Tempest* (BBC Radio 3).

LEAH BYRNE | Caitlin

Theatre credits include: *A Potted Christmas Carol*, *Oor Wullie*, *A–Z of Dundee* and *Tay Bridge* (all for Dundee Rep); *San Diego*, *Humbug!*, *The Breathing House*, *Orpheus & Eurydice*, *Strucken Moon*, *Julius Caesar*, *Philistines*, *Middletown*, *The Big Adventure* (all Royal Conservatoire of Scotland); *Whose Shoes?*, *Freckleface Strawberry: The Musical* and *Killing Me Softly* (all SYT Productions).

Film, Television and Audio Drama credits include: *Flaps* (Comedy Central); *Deadwater Fell* (Kudos/Channel 4); *The Last Bus* (Hurricane Films); *Call the Midwife, Fried, Whenever I Get Blown Up I Think of You* (BBC).

Leah trained at the Royal Conservatoire of Scotland.

PETER FORBES | Christopher

Theatre credits for the Royal Lyceum Theatre Edinburgh: *A Number* and *Educating Agnes*.

Other theatre credits include: *Follies, Our Country's Good, The Observer, Afterlife, Never So Good, Two Weeks with the Queen* (National Theatre of Great Britain); *The James Plays* (National Theatre of Scotland/National/tour); *Black Watch* (National Theatre of Scotland/Broadway/Dublin/tour); *Singin' in the Rain, Mamma Mia!, Henceforward...* (West End); *Allelujah!* (Bridge Theatre); *How to Hold Your Breath* (Royal Court); *The Same Deep Water as Me* (Donmar); *A Journey to London, Adam Bede* (Orange Tree); *The Winter's Tale, Troilus and Cressida* (Globe); *My Dad's a Birdman* (Young Vic); *A Midsummer Night's Dream, Twelfth Night, A Funny Thing Happened on the Way to the Forum, The Comedy of Errors, The Tempest* (Regent's Park Open Air Theatre); *Way Upstream, A Small Family Business, A Word From Our Sponsor* (Chichester Festival Theatre); *Cat on a Hot Tin Roof* (ETT/Leicester Curve); *The Three Musketeers and the Princess of Spain* (ETT/Traverse); *Diary of a Nobody, Travels with My Aunt* (Royal & Derngate); *Yes, Prime Minister* (Theatre Clwyd); *Treasure Island* (Rose, Kingston); *The Duchess of Malfi* (Mercury, Colchester); *Richard III, Aladdin, Juno and the Paycock, Guys and Dolls* (Haymarket, Leicester); *Donkeys' Years* (UK tour)

Film, Television and Audio Drama credits include: *Judy, The Children Act, The Wife, Modern Life is Rubbish, Nativity 3, Wilde, Blue Ice, Traces, Stephen, Manhunt, Poldark, King Lear, The Crown, Victoria, Endeavour, Holby City, Doctors, The Promise, The First Men in the Moon, EastEnders, Taggart, Little Devil, Bad Girls, The Bill, A Touch of Frost, The Government Inspector, Casualty, The English Revolution, Walking on the Moon, The Stalker's Apprentice, Berkeley Square, Behind Closed Doors – Life Chances, The Fortune of War, The Architects, Burns and the Bankers, Black Watch, Beryl Du Jour, Two Weeks with the Queen, Raffles*.

NEVE McINTOSH | Luci

Theatre credits for the Royal Lyceum Theatre Edinburgh: *The Merchant of Venice*.

Other theatre credits include: *Mouthpiece* (Traverse/Soho Theatre); *Killer Joe* (Trafalgar Studios); *Meet Me at Dawn* (Traverse Theatre); *The Crucible* (Bristol Old Vic); *The Events* (Edinburgh and New York); *Betrayal* (Citizens Theatre); *The*

Lady from the Sea (Royal Exchange Theatre); *Proof, Run for Your Wife, When We Were Women* (Perth Theatre); *Great Expectations, Victoria* (RSC); *The Recruiting Officer* (Lichfield Theatre); *Don Juan* (Sheffield Crucible); *Outside on the Street* (The Gate); *The Trick is to Keep Breathing* (Tron Theatre); *The Barber of Seville* (Arches Theatre).

Film and Television credits include: *Social Suicide, The Be All and End All, Spring 1941, One Last Chance, Gypsy Woman, The Trouble With Men and Women, Plunkett & Macleane, The Leading Man, Shetland, Tin Star, Traces, Stan Lee's Lucky Man, Guerilla, The Replacement, Death in Paradise, Critical, Ripper Street, Dracula, Doctor Who, Case Histories, The Accused, Single Father, Inspector George Gently, Sea of Souls, Low Winter Sun, Ghost Squad, Miss Marple, Bodies, Inspector Lynley Mysteries, Trial & Retribution, The Hound of the Baskervilles, Doc Martin, The Fear, Lady Audley's Secret, Gormenghast, Psychos* and *Taggart*.

CREATIVE TEAM

ZINNIE HARRIS | Writer and Director

Zinnie Harris is a playwright, screenwriter and theatre director and is also an Associate Director at the Royal Lyceum Theatre Edinburgh.

Theatre writing credits include: *The Duchess (of Malfi)* and *Rhinoceros* (Royal Lyceum Theatre Edinburgh); *This Restless House* (Citizens Theatre/National Theatre of Scotland); *Meet Me at Dawn* (Traverse Theatre); *How to Hold Your Breath, Nightingale and Chase* (Royal Court Theatre); *The* Wheel (National Theatre of Scotland); *Further than the Furthest Thing* (National Theatre of Great Britain/Tron Theatre); *Midwinter, Solstice* (RSC); *Fall* (Traverse Theatre/RSC); *By Many Wounds* (Hampstead Theatre); *A Doll's House* (Donmar Warehouse).

Theatre directing credits include: *Lyceum Christmas Tales, The Duchess (of Malfi), A Number* (Royal Lyceum Theatre Edinburgh); *Gut* (Traverse Theatre/National Theatre of Scotland); *Tracks of the Winter Bear* (Traverse Theatre); *The Garden* (Sound Festival); *Midwinter, Solstice* (RSC); *Gilt* (7:84); *Dealer's Choice* (Tron Theatre).

Film and television includes: *A Glimpse, Partners in Crime, Spooks, Richard Is My Boyfriend, Born with Two Mothers.*

Awards: Zinnie has received multiple awards including the Peggy Ramsay Award, John Whiting Award and several Fringe First Awards. She was joint winner of the 2011 Amnesty International Freedom of Expression Award, won the CATS award for Best Director for her production of *A Number* at the Royal Lyceum Theatre Edinburgh, and Best New Play for *This Restless House*. Her play *Midwinter* won the Arts Foundation Fellowship Award.

TOM PIPER | Designer

Theatre credits include: *Lyceum Christmas Tales, Mrs Puntilla and Her Man Matti, The Duchess (of Malfi)* and *Rhinoceros* (Royal Lyceum Theatre Edinburgh); *Hay Fever* (Royal Lyceum Theatre Edinburgh/Citizens Theatre); *Endgame, King Lear, Hamlet, The Libertine, Nora* (Citizens Theatre); *Cyrano de Bergerac* (National Theatre of Scotland/Royal Lyceum Theatre Edinburgh/Citizens Theatre); *Pelléas Et Mélisande, Eugene Onegin* (Garsington Opera); *Frankenstein, Hedda Gabler* (Northern Stage); *iHo* (Hampstead Theatre); *Harrogate* (HighTide/Royal Court); *A Midsummer Night's Dream, Romeo and Juliet* (Royal Shakespeare Company/UK tour); *Carmen La Cubana* (Le Chatelet, Paris); *White Teeth* (Kiln); *Red Velvet* (West End/Tricycle Theatre/New York); *A Wolf in Snakeskin Shoes* (Tricycle Theatre); *The King's Speech* (Birmingham REP/Chichester Festival Theatre/UK tour); *Orfeo* (Royal Opera House); *Tamburlaine The Great* (Theatre for a New Audience, New York).

Other credits include: Tom designed *Blood Swept Lands* and *Seas of Red* at the Tower of London and received an MBE for services to Theatre and First World War commemorations. Other recent exhibitions include: *Alice: Curiouser and Curiouser*, *Winnie-the-Pooh*, *Curtain Up* (V&A, Lincoln Centre New York); *Shakespeare Staging the World* (British Museum). He was Associate Designer at the RSC for ten years and has designed over thirty productions for the company.

Awards: Tom won an Olivier Award for Best Costume Design for *The Histories* (RSC). He also received an award for Best Design, CATS, for *Twelfth Night* (Dundee Rep).

NIROSHINI THAMBAR | Composer and Sound Designer

Theatre credits include: *Hindu Times* (Sound Stage – Royal Lyceum Theatre Edinburgh/Pitlochry Festival Theatre); *Ghosts* (National Theatre of Scotland); *Here* (Curious Monkey/Northern Stage); *Gagarin Way* (Dundee Rep); *Home is Not the Place* (Annie George); *Secret Life of Suitcases* (Ailie Cohen Puppets); *Revolution Days* (Bijli Productions); *The Tempest* (Tron Theatre); *Helping Hands* (Pitlochry Festival Theatre).

Her residencies/commissions include: National Theatre of Scotland, Edinburgh Mela, Imaginate, Drake Music Scotland and Magnetic North Theatre. Her work has been in productions at the Edinburgh International Festival, Shubbak Contemporary Arts Festival, Edinburgh Festival Fringe and the Adelaide Fringe Festival. Further work includes Composer for the documentary film in development *The Album* (Sana Bilgrami/BofA Productions), Associate Director for the audio-led production *Niqabi Ninja* (Independent Arts Projects), and Series Composer for *United Kingdoms* (Naked Productions/BBC Radio 4).

BEN OMEROD | Lighting Designer

Theatre credits for the Royal Lyceum Theatre Edinburgh: *The Duchess (of Malfi)*, *A Number*.

Other recent theatre credits include: *A Christmas Carol, A Long Day's Journey into Night, The Oresteia, Hamlet, King Lear* (Citizens Theatre, Glasgow); *Don Juan* (Perth Theatre); *Footfalls/Rockaby* (Jermyn Street Theatre); *The Dresser, A Song at Twilight* (Bath and UK tour); *Vienna 1934-Munich 1938, The Model Apartment, Trouble in Mind* (Ustinov Theatre Bath); *Mr Kipps* (Mountview); *The Sunset Limited* (Boulevard Theatre); *Assassins* (Watermill Newbury and Nottingham Playhouse); *Prism* (Birmingham Rep, UK tour); *Uncle Vanya, Prism, Loyalty* (Hampstead Theatre); *Broken Glass, The Dresser* (Watford Palace Theatre); *All's Well That Ends Well* (Sam Wanamaker Playhouse); *A Midsummer Night's Dream* (Regent's Park Open Air Theatre); *Zorro* (West End, Holland, Paris, US and Japan).

Other Credits: Opera includes *The Ring Cycle, Tristan and Isolde* (Longborough Festival); *La Traviata* (Danish National Opera); *Jeanna D'arc au Bûcher* (Academia Santa Cecilia, Rome); *Falstaff, Il Trovatore*, (Scottish Opera); *La Traviata* (English National Opera); *The Elixir of Love* (Norfolk Into Opera Festival).

Dance credits include: *The Shadow* (Company Chameleon); *@Home, The Knot* (Humanoove, UK tour); *Carmen* (EICC Edinburgh); *Is to Be* (Le Prix De Lausanne); *The Nutcracker, Les Noces* (Ballet Geneva); *Frame of View* (Cedar Lake Contemporary Ballet, New York); *See Blue Through/Toot!* (Oper Leipzig); *Tenderhooks* (Skanes Dansteater/Ballet Gulbenkian); *Essence* (Walker Dance Park Music).

Ben is also lighting designer for the Calico Museum of Textiles, Ahmedabad, directed Athol Fugard's *Dimetos* (Gate, London) and adapted four films from Kieslowski's *Dekalog* for E15.

WHITE & GIVAN | Movement Directors

Davina Givan and Errol White are award-winning dancers and performers with over thirty years' experience working with many acclaimed companies that include Richard Alston, Phoenix Dance Theatre, Scottish Dance Theatre and National Dance Company of Wales.

Recent theatre credits as Movement Directors include: *Swallow, Tracks of the Winter Bear, Milk, Grain the Blood, Girl in the Machine* (Traverse Theatre); and *Meet Me at Dawn* by Zinnie Harris (Edinburgh International Festival).

White & Givan's own dance productions include *Three Works* (2009); *IAM* (2012); *Breathe* (2014 and 2016–17 UK tour); and *Worn* (2020 film, touring Autumn 2022).

KAITLIN HOWARD | Fight Director

Kaitlin qualified as a Stage Combat instructor in 2005, is a founding member of The Academy of Performance Combat and is one of only three women on the Equity Register of Fight Directors.

Theatre credits include: *Life is a Dream* (Royal Lyceum Theatre Edinburgh); *Guards at the Taj* (Theatre by the Lake, Keswick); *A Midsummer Night's Dream, Our Country's Good* (Tobacco Factory, Bristol); *The Effect, A Skull in Connemara, Jack and the Beanstalk, Aladdin* (Oldham Coliseum); *The Merry Wives of Windsor* (Storyhouse, Chester); *Hushabye Mountain, A Kidnapping, Orphans, The Trial, The Pride, Hamlet* (Hope Mill Theatre, Manchester); *Twelfth Night, Arcadia, The Illusion* (HOME, Manchester); *The Sweet Science of Bruising, Blue Stockings, Playhouse Creatures* (Capitol Theatre, Manchester); *Posh, Decades, Game, Alice in Wonderland, Treasure Island, Scuttlers* (Wigan Pier); *Robin Hood* (Cast, Doncaster); *Drych* (Theatr Genedlaethol Cymru); *Romeo and Juliet*,

Macbeth (Epstein Theatre, Liverpool); *The Little Mermaid* (Liverpool Everyman); *The Comedy of Errors* (Greenwich Playhouse); *Killer Joe* (Pleasance Theatre, London).

Film and TV Fight Direction includes: *So Awkward Series 3 & 4*, *Crimewatch*, *Clouds*.

VANESSA COFFEY | Intimacy Director

Vanessa is a UK-based Intimacy Coordinator for screen and stage.

Intimacy Coordination credits for theatre include: *The Panopticon* (National Theatre of Scotland); *Anatomy of a Suicide*, *San Diego* and *Dead Man Walking* (Royal Conservatoire of Scotland).

TV/Film credits include: *I Hate Suzie* and *Wolfe* (Sky); *Outlander Series 6* (Starz); *Vikings: Valhalla* (MGM/Netflix) and *Rules of the Game* (BBC).

Alongside her work, Vanessa has contributed to the Directors UK Guidelines: Directing Nudity andSimulated Sex, and founded the Intimacy Practitioners' Guild (IPG) alongside fellow industry professionals.

SIMONE PEREIRA HIND CDG and ANNA DAWSON | Casting Directors

Simone's Theatre credits include: *The Ride Down Mount Morgan* for Arthur Miller, and *Twelve Angry Men* for Harold Pinter, with her sister Vanessa Pereira and the Royal Lyceum Theatre Edinburgh's opening post-pandemic production *Life is a Dream*.

Other recent credits include: feature films *Munich: The Edge of War* for Netflix, *Nobody Has to Know*, *Falling for Figaro*, *The Toll* and *Moon Dogs*. Simone also cast many features including *Elizabeth*, *Hamlet*, *Hilary and Jackie*, *Jude* and *Welcome to Sarajevo* whilst based in London.

Simone and Anna are responsible for the casting in Scotland of 6 series of *Outlander* and *Good Omens 2* for BBC/Amazon. They recently co-cast BBC Scotland series *Float*.

THEATRE MADE IN EDINBURGH

ARTISTIC DIRECTOR **DAVID GREIG**
EXECUTIVE DIRECTOR **MIKE GRIFFITHS**

The Royal Lyceum Theatre Edinburgh is the leading producing theatre in Scotland and one of the United Kingdom's most prolific theatre companies.

Our beautiful, intimate Victorian theatre was built in 1883 and has played a significant role in the cultural and creative life of the city and surrounding area for over 130 years. Since 1965, the current Lyceum company has developed a reputation for innovative, highquality theatre, drawing upon the considerable talent in Scotland as well as developing awardwinning work with partners across the globe to make theatre in Edinburgh that can speak to the world.

We believe that making and watching theatre together is life enhancing. We are committed to being a theatre rooted in our community, a truly civic theatre entertaining, challenging and inspiring all the people of Edinburgh. To reach the widest possible audience we find new ways to open our doors and stage to the public, as well as reaching out into Edinburgh's schools and neighbourhoods with a range of programmes taking place beyond our walls.

Under Artistic Director David Greig, The Lyceum has continued to seek out new artistic partnerships, casting 100 local citizens in our main stage production of *The Hour We Knew Nothing of Each Other* and 50 more in *The Suppliant Women*, the acclaimed production that opened David's first season. Since then we have made work with Malthouse Theatre, Melbourne; DOT Theatre, Istanbul; Bristol Old Vic; National Theatre of Scotland; Citizens Theatre; Scottish Dance Theatre; Stellar Quines; Lung Ha and Fuel.

For the latest information about The Lyceum visit **lyceum.org.uk**

ALBA | CHRUTHACHAIL

Royal Lyceum Theatre Company is a Scottish Charity
Registered No. SC010509

LYCEUM STAFF

Cameron Banks FOH Assistant
Lindsey Bell Deputy Head of Lighting and Sound
Sally Berry FOH Assistant
Jules Bilger General Technician
Sandy Bishop FOH Assistant
Oliver Bisset Theatre in Residence Drama Artist
Jane Black FOH Assistant
Hannah Bradley Duty Manager (FOH)
Gillian Brook Stage Door/Fire/Security
Adam Brook Stage Door/Fire/Security
Anna Brooke FOH Assistant
Connor Buchanan Finance Officer
David Butterworth Production Manager
Robert Castle FOH Assistant
Elspeth Chapman BO Assistant
Anthony Christie FOH Assistant
Jamie Cook FOH Assistant
Jackie Crichton Literary Associate
Jason Dailly Head of Workshop
Stephen Dennehy Box Office Manager
Daniel Dixon Company Stage Manager
Christine Dove Running Wardrobe
Tony Duff Stage Technician
Gavin Dunbar Box Office Supervisor
Jaime Foster Director of Finance & Admin
Julia Fraser Duty Manager
Katie Fraser Duty Manager
Lesley Gardner PA to the Chief Executives
Victoria Garner Duty Manager (FOH)
Yesica Garrido HR Officer
Ian Gibson Head of Lighting and Sound
Amie Gilbertson FOH Assistant
Russell Gray Maintenance Cleaner
David Greig Artistic Director & Chief Executive
Mike Griffiths Executive Director & Chief Executive
Joe Harper Buildings Maintenance and Services Manager
Zinnie Harris Associate Director
Fiona Harvey Director of Estates and Facilities
Kikelomo Hassan FOH Assistant
Meagan Hearons FOH Assistant
Georgina Heriot FOH Assistant
John Heron Stage Technician/Flyman
Caitlin Higgins BO Assistant
Emma Hindle FOH Assistant
Sophie Howell Creative Learning Officer
Adam James Duty Manager
Ben Jeffries Director of Communications
Heather Johns Creative Learning Officer
Russell Kemp BO Assistant
Liz King Director of Producing

Zoe King Assistant Stage Manager
Laura Kwiatkowski FOH Assistant
Catherine Leiper Stage Door/Fire/Security
Adam Lloyd FOH Assistant
Claire Loughran Stage Door/Fire/Security
Fereuse MacDonald Develoment & Database Administrator
Sharon May Head of Creative Learning
Kevin McAndrew Buildings Maintenance Technician
Ciara McCafferty Producer
Ross McFarlane Deputy Head of Lighting and Sound
Malcolm McQuillan Maintenance Cleaner
Amy McVicar FOH Assistant
Hamish Millar Head of Stage
Katie Miller BO Assistant
Rowan Milne FOH Assistant
Jessica Moran Duty Manager
Harriet Mould EDI Associate
Kalvin Moyes FOH Assistant
Ross Nisbet BO Assistant
Jaïrus Obayomi FOH Assistant
Jack Oliver FOH Assistant
Maria Papageorgiou FOH Assistant
Debi Pirie FOH Assistant
Leila Price Creative Learning Intern
Tim Primrose Stage Door/Fire/Security
Iain Ramponi Technical Manager
Simon Read Box Office Supervisor
Jessi Rich BO Assistant
Scott Ringan FOH Assistant
Mairi Rosko Development Director
Argyro Sapsouzli Costume Maker
Katie Schmieg Miller BO Assistant
Clare Sherwin FOH Assistant
Chantal Short FOH Assistant
Ross Sibbald Maintenance Cleaner
Darren Simpson FOH Assistant
Stephen Sinclair General Technician
Karen Sorley Costume Cutter
Lindsay Spear Theatre in Residence Drama Artist
Katie Stephen Duty Manager
Kelsey Stevenson Assistant Management Accountant
Jack Summers-McKay Events Manager
Chris Townsend FOH Assistant
Kerrie Walker Creative Learning Producer
Emma White Box Office Supervisor
Caitlin Wiedenhof Head of Costume
Claire Williamson Deputy Stage Manager
Wils Wilson Associate Director
Grazyna Wysocka Costume Maker
Josie Young Creative Learning Intern

The Scent of Roses

Zinnie Harris's plays include the multi-award-winning
Further than the Furthest Thing (National Theatre/Tron
Theatre; winner of the 1999 Peggy Ramsay Award, 2001
John Whiting Award, Edinburgh Fringe First Award), *How
to Hold Your Breath* (Royal Court Theatre; joint winner of
the Berwin Lee Award), *The Wheel* (National Theatre of
Scotland; joint winner of the 2011 Amnesty International
Freedom of Expression Award, Fringe First Award),
Nightingale and Chase (Royal Court Theatre), *Midwinter*,
Solstice (both RSC), *Fall* (Traverse Theatre/RSC), *By Many
Wounds* (Hampstead Theatre), the trilogy *This Restless
House*, based on Aeschylus' *Oresteia* (Citizens
Theatre/National Theatre of Scotland; Best New Play,
Critics Award for Theatre in Scotland) and *Meet Me at
Dawn* (Traverse Theatre). She has also adapted Ibsen's *A
Doll's House* for the Donmar Warehouse, Strindberg's *Miss
Julie* for the National Theatre of Scotland, *(the fall of) The
Master Builder* for Leeds Playhouse, and *The Duchess (of
Malfi)* for the Royal Lyceum Theatre, Edinburgh. She
received an Arts Foundation Fellowship for playwriting,
and was Writer in Residence at the RSC, 2000–2001. She is
the Professor of Playwriting and Screenwriting at the
University of St Andrews and an Associate Director at the
Royal Lyceum Theatre in Edinburgh.

ZINNIE HARRIS

The Scent of Roses

faber

First published in 2022
by Faber and Faber Limited
74–77 Great Russell Street, London WC1B 3DA

Typeset by Brighton Gray
Printed and bound in the UK by CPI Group (Ltd), Croydon CR0 4YY

A CIP record for this book
is available from the British Library

ISBN 978-0-571-37602-5

2 4 6 8 10 9 7 5 3 1

The Scent of Roses was first performed at the Royal Lyceum Theatre, Edinburgh, on 25 February 2022. The cast, in alphabetical order, was as follows:

Saskia Ashdown Sally
Maureen Beattie Helen
Leah Byrne Caitlin
Peter Forbes Christopher
Neve McIntosh Luci

Writer and Director Zinnie Harris
Designer Tom Piper
Composer and Sound Designer Niroshini Thambar
Lighting Designer Ben Ormerod
Movement Directors White & Givan
Fight Director Kaitlin Howard
Intimacy Director Vanessa Coffey
Casting Directors Simone Pereira Hind CDG
  and Anna Dawson
Company Stage Manager Owen Thomas
Deputy Stage Manager Claire Williamson
Assistant Stage Manager Jessica Ward
Set Builders Splinter Scenery
Wardrobe Supervisor Morag Pirrie
Script Associate Jackie Crichton

Characters

Luci
Christopher
Caitlin
Sally
Helen

THE SCENT OF ROSES

Part One

ONE

A bedroom.

Chest of drawers.

Nice things.

Christopher stands by the bed. Luci by the window.

Luci
you don't know yet

Beat.

do you?
when you go in tomorrow, you'll hear more, but until
then –

Christopher
what?
be positive?

Luci
well just –

Christopher
nah, when it starts to go like this

Luci
you don't know

Christopher
I do know
there's a smell, an odour
remember that other case – McPherson something, it's
the same as that

Luci

what does Ollie say?

Christopher

he doesn't know any more than me
and I know it should be good, it's a good thing, of course
to settle but without the day in court – when does it get
said?
when does all the work get seen?

Beat.

She comes over to him.

Luci

I'm sorry.

Kisses the top of his head.

Christopher

ach. It's just a dream isn't it. The case that everyone
remembers.
but do you ever actually get that? Probably not.

Luci

anything I can do?

Christopher

take me out, buy me a steak!

Luci

done.

Christopher

really?

Luci

why not?

Christopher

alright. You know the worst, the worst is all that time.
All those interviews, all those miserable stories of people
screwed over, years I've been at this

Luci
there'll be another one

Christopher
have I got the energy for it though?
to start again?
Ollie says there is another one coming

Luci
well, get that –

Christopher
Sanderson's got it
we'll not get a sniff.
that's the real fucker. The law might have to change but
not because of the work I put in.

He looks at her.

the law *will* change
it's how it works, someone else will get the credit

Luci
it's shit

Christopher
ach, it's how it is
I'll drink a couple of gins I'll be fine
bollocks to it Luci

Luci
exactly
bollocks to it

Beat.

Christopher
I don't know if I can be bothered going out actually

Luci
really?

Christopher
what about takeaway?

Luci
can you get a takeaway steak?

Christopher
you can get takeaway anything can't you, but no I meant
– anything really.
I probably just want to get pissed
what do you think, shall we stay in?
go to bed or something

Luci
go to bed

Christopher
I didn't mean go to bed, I just meant –

Luci
oh

Christopher
I mean I wouldn't mind going to bed, I just meant –
I didn't mean anything but –

Luci
I could go to bed

Beat.

Christopher
could you?

Beat.

I might be a bit off par mind you
bit pissed off, bit miserable
bit lacking

Luci
unlikely.

He sits down on the bed.

Reaches out to her.

Christopher
or we could make do with a cuddle

Luci
that would be fine too

Christopher
how was your day?

Luci
uneventful by comparison, just kind of –
I sorted some stuff

Christopher
all this?

Luci
I was clearing out

Christopher
from where?

Luci
box in the attic

Christopher
weren't you at work?

Luci
came home at lunchtime, had a headache

Christopher
that isn't uneventful

Luci
slight headache, nothing
probably the heat

Christopher
    Luci?

Luci
    I'd tell if you there was anything going on
    just a headache, nothing

Beat.

He lies down on the bed.

Christopher
    worst of it is, I'd got all the publicity lined up. Papers,
    Newsnight, I think we would have had it all –

Luci
    you don't know it's off yet –

Christopher
    I do really.
    I know how it goes from here

She comes and puts her arms around him. Kisses him.

Luci
    wait and hear what Ollie says in the morning.
    you never know, you might be surprised

He holds her hand.

Christopher
    you're my hero

Luci
    you lie

Christopher
    not at all. I think you're wonderful.

He kisses her.

She kisses him.

He kisses her again.

She kisses him again.

The possibility of more is hovering.

Luci
 Caitlin said she might come over at some point
 just so you know

Christopher
 oh
 this evening?

Luci
 she thought about eight –

Christopher
 what time is it now?

Luci
 not sure . . . seven-ish?

Beat.

 mind you with Caitlin, around eight is anytime

Christopher
 bugger
 and she's got a key, she could walk in unannounced

Luci
 she rings the bell now

Christopher
 she rings the bell?

Luci
 yes

Christopher
 when did that start?

Luci
 since she doesn't live here anymore!

Christopher
and if we don't answer?

Luci
then she'll use her key

Christopher
little fucker

Luci
but at least we'll have some warning.

He looks at her.

Christopher
remember when she walked in on us when she was about four?

Luci
three.

Christopher
three.

Luci
and seven and once again when she was nine.

Christopher
oh yes when she was nine.
in the garden

They giggle for a second.

He kisses her again.

wasn't there something we were supposed to be doing tonight?

Luci
doesn't matter

Christopher
some work thing for you?

Luci
not important

Christopher
you sure?

Luci
they happen all the time, no one even notices if I'm not there.

Christopher
I love you.

Luci
I know.

He kisses her.

Christopher
just to warn you, I had a couple of gins on the way home so I might be a bit –

She laughs.

Luci
when did I mind that?

Christopher
fuck off.

He kisses her again.

tell me it's not a pity fuck

Luci
it's not a pity fuck.

TWO

Later.

Christopher and Luci are lying in bed.

Christopher
tea?

Luci
nah.

Christopher
gin?

Luci
in a minute

Christopher
I need to move my back
hang on
shit my knees

Luci
no fun getting old

Christopher
speak for yourself.

He hugs in.

that was lovely.
you are lovely.

They lie there for a second.

what is Caitlin coming over for anyway?

Luci
you know Caitlin, she might not even turn up.

Christopher
what does she want?

Luci

don't say it like that

Christopher

I didn't mean –

Luci

she does still live here really, all her stuff is here

Christopher

I know but –

Luci

she needs a backpack I think. She wants to go camping at the weekend, and I said she could borrow whatever she wanted

Christopher

who with?

Luci

she's nineteen, I wasn't going to ask her who with. You should be more worried about what state the attic is in

Christopher

what state is the attic in?

Luci

pretty ropey.
like us

Christopher

fuck off.

Luci

you started it.

Christopher

you feeling hungry yet, at all?

Luci

not sure

Christopher
quite fancy a steak now –

Luci
see that up there

Christopher
where?

Luci
that smudge on the ceiling, that mark

Christopher
we had it dealt with

Luci
we thought we did
I think the attic might be leaking again
there's a stain

He comes and looks at it.

Christopher
we'll get them back in

Luci
or we could leave it

Christopher
what?

Luci
it's quite interesting
the shape it makes. Its unapologetic nature.

He looks at it.

Then he looks at her.

He kisses her again.

Christopher
you've gone light-headed.
steak!

He starts to get up.

Luci
can we go in a minute, can we talk

Christopher
we are talking

Beat.

aren't we talking?

Luci
we are talking, but I need to talk more

Christopher
talk more or talk *more*?

Luci
talk *more*

Christopher
it wasn't just a headache?

Luci
it was just a headache

Christopher
you've found another lump

Luci
no

Christopher
you promise?

Luci
yes, I promise.

He gets up, he puts pants on.

Trousers.

She watches him.

Christopher
sorry, you mean you want to talk in bed?

Luci
I know you want your steak, but you don't have to rush off

Christopher
I'm not rushing anywhere, fine if you want to stay and talk but I'm going to get a drink first

Luci
the door is locked

Christopher
what?

Luci
I locked the door

Christopher
when?

Luci
before

Christopher
before?

Luci
when you came in

Christopher
well open it

Luci
I locked the door because I need to talk to you

Christopher
and we can't do that over dinner?

Luci
we could but I'd prefer to do it here.

Christopher
we talk all the time

Luci
we do talk to each other technically yes but

Christopher
alright, open the door and we'll talk

Luci
no

Christopher
you can't literally lock the door on me

Luci
I did

Christopher
well you might've done, but you can't

Luci
there's no point saying I can't when I have. I did it

Christopher
are you actually joking?

Luci
no

Christopher
so, where's the key?

Luci
I'm not telling you, clearly I'm not telling you, I locked the door why would I tell you where the key was?

Christopher
you're locking me in a room?

Luci
our bedroom yes, with me

Christopher

that's imprisonment

Luci

well okay. It's imprisonment then

Christopher

I don't understand what's going on, Luci

Luci

for god's sake, I locked the door because I want to have a
conversation, not to incarcerate you for ever

Christopher

no, you locked the door because you wanted to have a
certain *type* of conversation and you knew I might not

Luci

alright

Christopher

and you thought that there was a fair chance I'd be tired
I might not be receptive, I guess you didn't count on my
work having gone tits up, but even without that you
didn't want to have to think that I might be a person
with my own agenda who might not want to have any
kind of conversation right now, and that I also have a
choice.

Luci

well you don't now

Christopher

I do. You can lock me in a room, I don't have to talk to
you.

Luci

oh, I see. It's me that's being ridiculous?

He goes and checks the door. It's locked.

I didn't think I'd be able to do it actually. It's a funny
thing –
I thought about this all afternoon, while I was in bed
with a headache looking at that stain

Christopher
you thought about it all afternoon?

Luci
yes

Christopher
whoa. You've been *planning* this?

Luci
you'd be surprised how a simple thing like locking up
your husband in the same room as you, makes you aware
of something. Alive. It's a kind of new thing to do isn't it,
a stepping off. I've never locked you in a room before.
this will go into the new lexicon. Things we can do to
each other.

Christopher
only we can't

Luci
but I have.

Beat.

Christopher
I'm not talking to you while I am locked in.
that isn't how this is going to work

Luci
well we'll be staying here for a long while then.
up to you.

Christopher
you're being even more crazy than normal, you realise
that?

Luci

and I knew you'd say that. I knew you'd use those exact words.

Christopher

didn't we just make love back there?

Luci

if someone had said to me, how do you think your husband will react when you lock him in a room, I could have told them, he'll say I'm crazy

Christopher

you are though.

Luci

or maybe I'm being really sane. For the first time in ages.

Christopher gets fully dressed.

He goes over and kicks the door.

you make it out like it's a crime, that talking is –

Christopher

holding me against my wishes is, not listening when I say I don't want to talk to you.

Luci

an actual crime?

Christopher

yep

Luci

a judge would rule that?

He kicks the door again.

Christopher

this door shouldn't even lock –

Luci

would a judge rule that?

Christopher
I don't know what a judge would rule

Luci
when the builder came last year, he found a key, I thought it might be useful

Christopher
last year?

Luci
I didn't know I would need it then, I just thought –

Christopher
I think I'm going to get claustrophobic

Luci
oh I see

Christopher
what happens if I actually get claustrophobic, have a panic attack?

Luci
I'll tell you not to be so stupid

Christopher
have you thought of that, though?

Luci
I didn't imagine that in my series of scenarios, no

Christopher
in your *planning*?

Luci
no because I think of you as a reasonable person who can probably cope with being in his own bedroom

Christopher
I am, I am actually feeling really weird

Luci
for fuck's sake Christopher

Christopher
you know I don't like being in enclosed spaces

Luci
when did you ever tell me that?

He sits down, puts his head between his knees.

you've never said that, never in twenty-one years
if you pass out I will stick your feet up.

Christopher
shit I feel awful

Luci
oh, this is a real thing?

Christopher
I think I am going to pass out
I'm actually getting a bit panicky
please don't do this

Luci
but I have done it, haven't I? I can't *not* do this now
because I have started.

He puts his head in his hands.

She stands up. She puts a dressing gown on.

She gets a glass of water.

She hands it to him.

He drinks it.

better?

Christopher
no.

Luci
you won't pass out. Twenty-one years you've never
passed out.

some people just aren't passer-outers.
sorry.

He sits there for a minute.

He does in fact feel fine.

He goes to his jacket pocket.

He looks through; panicked, he goes to the other pocket.

Christopher
you've taken my phone

Luci
yes

Christopher
you took my phone?

Luci
yes, you just asked me

Christopher
you took my phone and then you locked me in a room?

Luci
there was no point locking you in a room if you could
just phone someone to get you out.

Christopher
just so we could talk?

Luci
imagine how desperate to have a conversation with you
I must be!

Christopher
do you have your phone?

Luci
no

Christopher
so, we're in a locked room without either phone?

Luci
I think we'll survive

Christopher
but if I did have a panic attack or some medical
emergency, you couldn't even get us help?

Luci
you're making too much of this

Christopher
I have rights

Luci
oh okay

Christopher
everyone has a right not to be held against their will

Luci
well you should know

Christopher
will you open this door Luci?

Luci
no

Christopher
will you open this door Luci?

Luci
no

Christopher
Luci open this door

Luci
no

Christopher
open the door

Luci
no

Christopher
Luci –

Luci
no

Christopher
Luci –

Luci
no

Christopher
Luci –

Beat.

well I mean is there a time frame to this, how long are
you going to keep me in here?

Luci
that depends

Christopher
on?

Luci
on you

Christopher
on me?

Luci
yes

Christopher
because it seems like the whole thing depends on you

Luci
not at all. Anyway, what about my rights, don't I have
rights?

Christopher

not really in this situation

Luci

do I not have a right to talk to my husband?

Christopher

no

Luci

not even if there is stuff that we need to talk about?

Christopher

I can't actually think of a situation where someone has successfully claimed that they had a *right* to get someone else to speak. Plus I haven't even eaten anything yet, could you not have waited until after dinner to pull this little stunt?

Luci

it wouldn't have had the impact

Christopher

fuck's sake.
I'm starving.
I'm really hungry

Luci

you poor thing

Luci stands up, she goes to a drawer and she gets out a plate of food that she already prepared.

there you go

Christopher

holy shit.

She takes the plate over and puts it in front of him.

He looks at it.

THREE

Christopher is toying with the food on the plate.

Christopher
wedding anniversary, someone's birthday?

Luci
no

Christopher
anniversary of your mother's death?

Luci
no

Christopher
well I must have missed something –

Luci shakes her head.

He looks back at the plate.

I thought we were past this

Luci
I thought we were too

Christopher
all the dramatics, all that stuff.

Luci
yep

He pushes the meal away.

Christopher
well go on then, start

Luci
if you're ready, then okay –

Christopher
isn't that the point. I'm not ready.
you made me captive.

you can't make me captive and then say I have to be
ready.
it's like saying someone has to enjoy something while
beating them over the head.
but yes, go on.

She takes something out of her pocket.

Luci
I didn't choose today to talk to you. Today happened
with its own timing. That's the first thing I need to say.

Christopher
what does that mean?

Luci
I found something

Christopher
where?

Luci
in the attic

Christopher
okay
where in the attic?

Luci
on our old computer
I suppose near the leak

She gives him a piece of paper.

He unfolds it.

Christopher
I can't read it, I haven't got my glasses

Luci
here are your glasses

She passes him his glasses case.

36

Christopher
Caitlin will come eventually

Luci
she doesn't have a key

Christopher
she does have a key

Luci
not to this room

Christopher
she will call someone, she is sensible
we won't be stuck in here once Caitlin arrives

Luci
true

Christopher
so really all I have to do is sit it out

Luci
why don't you look at it?

Christopher
because I think it is likely to bite me.

Beat.

Christopher takes his glasses and starts to put them on.

did you know – I'm just asking the question – did you
know that the tennis is on tonight?

Luci
I didn't

Christopher
it's the semi-final

Luci
so

Christopher

it's the US Open men's semi-final

Luci

you thought we were going out tonight so you wouldn't have watched it anyway –

Christopher

I was hoping we would get back and watch the end

Luci

you don't even like tennis

Christopher

fuck's sake

Luci

okay well you tell me, you never did
tennis is boring

Christopher

why don't you tell me what I am. I have watched tennis for years

Luci

not years

Christopher

years

Luci

alright yes technically years, but not *years* when you say it like that, it sounds like *decades*

Christopher

you tell me then

Luci

you used to hate it, when we were first together, that's the thing. All sport but especially tennis.

Christopher

am I not allowed to change?

Luci
but you used to go on about it, what a momentous waste of time it was, all that backwards and forwards with the ball

Christopher
I changed

Luci
but why? and when?

Christopher
oh *that's* my crime?

Luci
it was one of the things that made us the same

Christopher
not liking tennis?

Luci
an ideological opposition to sport, yes

Christopher
people change
people evolve, Luci

Luci
okay, but when they do, you can normally see where it comes from

Christopher
you think it's phoney

Luci
I think it comes from someone else. Yes.

Christopher
ah okay

Beat.

I see now where we're headed.

Luci

I don't think it's your true nature

Christopher

but you don't give an arse about whether I watch tennis really

Luci

it's an example

Christopher

of my true nature

Luci

it's just odd

Christopher

which only you know?

Luci

I didn't say that

Christopher

you more or less did. Well go on, you said you think it comes from someone else, you might as well finish. Who?

Beat.

go on, who?

She doesn't say anything.

who?

Luci

you tell me

He looks at the piece of paper.

Christopher

didn't we agree, we wouldn't rake things up?

Luci

when did we ever agree that?

Christopher
it's kind of implied in moving on

Luci
oh I see, that's the implication

He reads the email.

He sits still for a minute.

She looks at him.

He looks at her.

He folds the piece of paper and hands it back to her.

She doesn't take it.

Christopher
well the first thing is, it's three years old

Luci
aha

Christopher
I don't even use that email account anymore

Luci
that isn't why I showed you

Christopher
why are you doing this, Luci?

Luci
because it needs to be done.

Christopher
it doesn't actually.

He reads it again.

He folds it away.

it's three years old

Luci

you already said that

He looks at her.

She looks at him.

Christopher

what are we doing here? In this locked room

Luci

we are talking

Christopher

oh is that what this is?

Beat.

FOUR

Christopher is striding across the room.

Luci is sitting.

Christopher

let me go downstairs and get a drink. I promise I will
come back up and we can go through it all, but please I
don't think I can do this as sober as I am.

Luci

you need to let go of the idea of being let out of here, this
obsession –

Christopher

for god's sake Luce. Just some wine. No games, I will talk
alright but please stop all this.

Luci

I'm not going to open the door

Christopher

what if I smashed the window and climbed out?

She looks at the window.

Luci

are you likely to?

Christopher

I'm just wondering if you thought of that?

Luci

I didn't particularly but the windows are double glazed

Christopher

I bet there's something in the bathroom I could smash
them with

Luci

we're three floors up here

Christopher

so?

Luci

so are you going to jump down three floors?
remember the fuss you made when we had to cross that
bridge

Christopher

I could shout
I could get someone's attention, I could throw things
down to the street

Luci

yes, I suppose you could

She looks at the window.

Christopher

didn't we once have a bottle of whisky in here?

Luci

did we?

Christopher

that time you had a sore tooth

Luci
I hate whisky

Christopher
I just need something to knock me out

He goes to the cupboard beside the bed.

Luci
it's not there now

Christopher
what about the bathroom?

Luci
I doubt it. I'm sorry I didn't bring up any wine for you

Christopher
or you –

Luci
no, I brought up wine for me

Christopher
what?

Luci
I thought I might need something to drink

Christopher
where is it?

Luci
well you won't like it

Christopher
I will drink anything just now

Luci
okay

She stands up.

She goes to the wardrobe.

She gets out a bottle of champagne.

She looks at him.

Christopher
what are you playing at?

Luci
I'm getting a drink

Christopher
that isn't just champagne, that is –

Luci
I know

Christopher
what the hell – ?

Luci
it's a good one

Christopher
fucking pricey one. Win the lottery one

Luci
well I was hoping to celebrate

Christopher
what?

Luci
that we'd finally had a conversation

They look at each other.

He gets up and grabs the wine off her.

Christopher
don't flinch I wasn't going to hit you
when have I ever hit you? Don't do that.
I'm only going to open the champagne

He opens the champagne.

He takes a long glug from the bottle.

Fucking bubbles, he has to wipe his mouth.

He hands it to her.

Changes his mind, takes a second long glug.

Gives it to her.

Changes his mind again. Drinks more.

She grabs it back.

Drinks some too.

He sits back down against the door.

you know you scare me sometimes

Luci
you can start by telling me in reality, what has gone on
for the last three years. What kind of universe we are
living in

Beat.

Christopher
maybe you should tell me what you want me to say?
write me a script

Beat.

I'm not denying anything.
have I denied anything?

Luci
that is an account I didn't even know you had. That's the
email saying, whatever it says in the other email is
wrong, I want to stay in touch

Christopher
her daughter was ill, she was in and out of trouble, I was
worried about her. That was it at first

Luci

and now? I want to know how it is *now*. How often do you see her? Weekly, daily, what is it?

Beat.

Christopher

you're going to pull this all down you know. Everything that we've got here

Luci

it's not me that's pulling it down

FIVE

Christopher has picked up a chair and is using it to try to bash through the door.

The chair does nothing.

He tries it again.

Christopher

you'd have thought she'd be here by now.
Caitlin? Hangs around for years then on the one night I could do with her –

Luci

are you going to smash everything in this room?

Christopher

maybe? Are you going to stop me?
or are you going to squirrel it away as another example of my inadequacy in some way? He didn't even manage to smash the door in. He couldn't even do that.
you know the thing about Helen, she doesn't do that. She doesn't judge me like that, she actually likes me.

Luci

I'm sure she does

Christopher
she does
she thinks I am bloody marvellous. She thinks I'm funny,
my breath is okay. I can cook a meal and she doesn't
comment. In fact she does and she says it's tasty. Tasty! In
fact better than tasty, delicious.
whereas you, it's burnt or it's cold or I mistimed it, or
somehow forgot something and you make me feel so
fucking small. I can't bear it. I can't bear it sometimes.
yes, I'm flawed, I'm really fucking flawed. I make
mistakes all the time. And yes, I am going to keep trying
to smash this even if I fucking fail. Oh for fuck's sake –

The chair breaks.

He throws it down.

He has hurt his hand.

fuck fuck shit

Luci
what is it?

Christopher
ahh jesus, this isn't funny

He has blood all over this hand.

look at that

Luci
I can see

Christopher
you see, this is a dangerous game

Luci
I need you to calm down

Christopher
while I'm bleeding to death?

Luci
you won't bleed to death

Christopher
please just open the door, and then I'll fuck off or divorce you or whatever you want

Luci
I want you to represent me

Christopher
what?

Luci
I need a lawyer. And a good one.

Christopher
what the fuck?

Luci comes over to him.

Luci
let me see this hand?
okay, yep needs a bandage

She finds something to bandage his hand with. A dress of hers.

He sits still.

She goes and gets some scissors, cuts the dress.

Christopher
don't you like that dress?

She shrugs.

Luci starts putting the fabric around his hand.

Luci
just say yes or no
I need representation

Christopher
it's not a good idea for a husband to represent his wife

Luci
it might not be a good idea, but it's what I'm asking

Christopher
well, what is the case?

Luci
I want to sue you for sex without consent

Christopher
what?

Luci
and I want you to accept it

Christopher
have you completely lost your mind?

Luci
it's a straightforward proposition

Christopher
but we haven't had sex without consent

Luci
I went to see a lawyer today

Christopher
I *am* a lawyer

Luci
I know but I had this feeling you wouldn't help me, so I went to see my own lawyer. Tell me about consent I said

Christopher
you consented, you can't tell me you didn't consent –

Luci
how many times do you think we've had sex?

Christopher
I have no idea
is that what he asked you?

Luci
she.
no, it is what I am asking you

Luci has finished the bandage, she ties it off.

how many times have we had sex in twenty-one years?

Christopher
I don't know

Luci
estimate

Christopher
hundreds, thousands maybe

Luci
how many times in the past three years?

Christopher
fair few

Luci
last week, last month?

Christopher
yes okay, we have frequent, consensual, mutually
satisfying sex

Luci
tell me about consent I said to the lawyer

Christopher
this isn't about consent

Luci
medical consent, let's start there I said. My husband knows
a lot about medical consent, he is a medical consent lawyer

Christopher

who did you see?

Luci

it doesn't matter who I saw

Christopher

was it someone I know?

Luci

as it happens I chose someone from the internet

Christopher

probably some idiot then

Luci

not an idiot at all

Christopher

you understand this is ridiculous

Luci

medical consent she said. Yes, I said, tell me

Christopher

you know about it

Luci

you've told me enough times, yes I know how your cases work. How this big case will work, oh – maybe our case will be the one to make your name?

Christopher

shut up

Luci

consent has to be *voluntary*, the patient has to have the *capacity to give consent* and they have to be *informed*. They have to know if the doctor has any vested interests elsewhere. Tell me again what your big case right now is about? Patients not being informed about the context.

Beat.

Christopher

sexual consent is completely different to medical consent
fucking hell, you have gone crazy

Luci

I'm just saying – was I informed about our context?

Beat.

Christopher

I won't do it

Luci

we'll make the papers, you'll get your case –

Christopher

fuck off
I'm a cheating bastard yes
I'll write that down if you like, but –

Luci

that's no good to me
I want to change the law, Chris.
I want everyone in my position to be protected, just as
they are medically

Christopher

you are so fucking dramatic, do you have to be so
explosive
you realise that sex without consent is rape?

Luci

yes I do.

SIX

He is cutting up her dresses, idly, without passion.

Luci
why are you doing that?

Christopher
because it makes me feel better.
I think it might be my new hobby
and because you have already lost your mind so –

Luci
please stop.

Christopher thinks about it for a second.

Christopher
sorry, no.
you did it first, it looked good.
it's almost midnight now, where the fuck is our daughter?

He carries on chopping.

every single husband or wife would be able to sue their
unfaithful spouse

Luci
possibly

Christopher
you want to turn the world upside down like that?

Luci
why not?

Christopher
what about fantasy – people have fantasies, what if you
were having sex with one person but thinking about
someone else, should you tell them?

Luci
it's not the same

Christopher

having sex with someone who is *thinking about someone else* is different to having sex with someone who is *thinking about you.*

Luci

you're degrading the argument

Christopher

where can we draw the line Luci? Or what about – hang on let me think – we have a fight, about say – I don't know, the bins, should the bins go out. You say you'll do it. You forget. Fair do's everyone forgets. Later I ask you, did you put the bins out, you say yes

Luci

I lie?

Christopher

we all lie about things like that, life isn't possible without those small lies. Yes you lie. And then we have sex. Can you say that was informed?

Luci

you had sex with me on the understanding that the bins had gone out?

Christopher

yes

Luci

sleeping with someone else is not the same as putting the bins out

Christopher

okay take today, our case in point. The sex we had this evening. What about me? My right to know the context. would I have had sex with you if I had known that hours later you would accuse me of rape? Certainly not. Would I have had sex if I had known you would lock the door and trap me here? No no no. Would I have even walked into this room with you?

Luci
that argument implies you have to know everything about someone before you can consent, which clearly –

Christopher
there is one question that has to be answered. Do you want to have sex with this person? Now in this moment.

Luci
no the point is, if you knew that the person you are deceiving *wouldn't* want to have sex if they knew the truth, then you've only got consent through deception.

Beat.

please don't chop that one.
you know that one is expensive –

Beat.

He pauses.

and my mother gave it to me

He chops it.

SEVEN

He is standing looking out of the window. The chair is broken by the door.

The champagne is finished.

Luci is cleaning her teeth in the bathroom.

Christopher
it's starting to get light again Luce

Luci
I don't care

Beat.

Christopher

clearly Caitlin didn't come.

not that that seems to bother you. Where is Caitlin, who cares.

I've got work this morning, who cares.

there is a whole world out there that we should be part of, who cares.

Luci spits and comes out.

Luci

what was wrong with her daughter?

Christopher

what?

Luci

you said there was something wrong with Helen's daughter, that's why you stayed in touch with her at first?

Christopher

please open the door

Luci

you have to stop asking

Christopher

what if I actually attacked you, did you actually think about that? You are working on a presumption that I am not a violent man.

Luci looks at him.

Luci

I'm probably the more violent of the two of us

Christopher

that depends.

Beat.

I've got something I want to ask you

Luci
go on then

Christopher
when were you going to tell me about this?

He gets out a sheet of paper out of his pocket.

Luci
what is it?

Christopher
my own revelation. Something I found.
your side of your bed.

Luci
when?

Christopher
just now
when you were in there –

She glances at it.

it's dated the fifth

She knows what it is without looking really.

Luci
it isn't the same

Christopher
were you going to tell me?

Luci
you shouldn't have found that

Christopher
two weeks you've had this letter
you do understand the hypocrisy?

Luci
I'm not having an affair with my cancer

Christopher

no but by not telling me it has come back, you are deceiving.

everything we are doing is on the basis of deception

Luci

I've broken no rule

Christopher

when were you going to tell me?

Luci

I wasn't

I wasn't

I was going to get better or die and let you find out then

Christopher

Luci

Luci

I can't stand you. I despise you.

Christopher

you still should have told me.

Beat.

Luci

what if I do kill you? What if I take these scissors?

Christopher

I would fight back

and I'm stronger

Luci

I'm probably angrier

and I know where to stick them

Christopher

so do I.

Beat.

They look at each other.

Luci
I'd start with your eyes, oddly. I'd like to see them gouged from their sockets.

Christopher
I'd put my hands around your neck

Luci
then I'd move from the eyes to the rest of the skull

Christopher
I'd throw you to the floor

Luci
I'd tear the hair from your scalp

Christopher
stamp on your face

Luci
crack open your chest

Christopher
lacerate your thighs

Luci
pour boiling water on your back

Christopher
chop off your hands and feet

Luci
and then when you were dead

Christopher
I'd spit on you.

Beat.

They look at each other.

I don't know why you are looking at me like that.

Luci
I don't know why you are looking at me like that

Beat.

Christopher
what have the doctors said?

Luci
I'm not talking to you about it.

Christopher
you can't go through it alone

Luci
I am alone.
I am blood and bone and most definitely alone.

Beat.

Helen told me it wasn't just her. She told me there were lots of women over the years.

Christopher
I am not talking about Helen anymore.

Beat.

let me help you through this?

Luci
I have friends

Christopher
I am your oldest one

Luci
you had sex with me without my consent. You don't do that to your friends.

Christopher
what about imprisonment?
entrapment?
deception about a major illness?

blackmail?
do you do that to your friends?

The doorbell rings.

Silence.

They sit there.

The doorbell rings again.

that's her
Caitlin
finally
that's our daughter. Luci.

Luci
I know it's our daughter.

They look at each other.

Part Two

ONE

A young woman stands with a bird in her hand.

She is covered in blood.

Caitlin
 I killed a bird

Sally
 what?

Caitlin
 I didn't mean to but, fuck
 I think it's dead

Sally isn't much older than Caitlin, early twenties. She stands in her pyjamas.

Sally
 jesus, are you okay?

Caitlin
 it was an accident, obviously it was an accident

Sally
 you're covered in blood –

Caitlin
 it's some sort of crow I think or maybe it's a blackbird
 can you take it?

Sally
 Caitlin –

Caitlin
 sorry

Sally
 what are you doing here?

Caitlin

I was just on my bike, I was outside your house

Sally

at this time of night?

Caitlin

I was on the road outside your house, obviously I wasn't
outside your house –
I wasn't going to come in, I wasn't even thinking about
coming in, I was just on your road and this thing flew
into me
I didn't mean to hurt it just

Sally

you cycled into a bird?

Caitlin

there must have been something wrong with it
you can't just kill a bird on a bike, can you?
can you kill a bird on a bike?

Sally

I don't know
put it down

Caitlin

I was just on your road I thought –

Sally

you're covered in blood

Caitlin

that's not my blood
it's not the bird's blood
I don't know what that blood is

Sally

it must be the bird's blood

Caitlin

do birds bleed?

Sally

is it definitely dead?

Caitlin

I don't know, it looks pretty dead
you look at it
maybe they carry diseases, birds?

Sally

maybe you should put it down

Caitlin

yes where?

Sally

here in the bin

Caitlin

I don't want to hold it anymore

Sally

well, put it down, put it down

Caitlin

I just think now it's dead

Sally

I'll get some paper, wrap it up

Caitlin

but it's my responsibility isn't it? I killed it. Maybe I
should have to hold it like this for the rest of my life

Sally

what?

Caitlin

it was fine and then now it's not. And even if I get a job,
I get all these amazing opportunities I will say sorry I
have to hold this bird, it's my penance for killing it. And
then I won't be able to do anything because I will just be
holding this bird so my life will pretty much be fucked

and I won't be able to eat or go to the toilet or wank or
roll a joint unless I learn to use my feet, which I could do
I suppose, I could grow fingers from my toes and –

Sally
Caitlin stop

Beat.

Caitlin
sorry Mrs Granger

Sally
I'd forgotten you were like this

Caitlin
Ms, Ms Granger

Sally
you never called me that

Caitlin
sorry Sally.
Sally.

Beat.

oh, shit you were about to go to bed

Sally
not really

Caitlin
you're in your pyjamas –

Sally
it doesn't matter

Caitlin
you don't need this bird crap do you?
you're being polite, but you are pretty tired and you
haven't seen me for years
you want to go to bed actually, you wish I would fuck off

Sally
yes but

Caitlin
why don't you say it then?

Beat.

Sally
I was on my way to bed, yes, but –
at least get the blood off you

Caitlin
you always were the kindest teacher

Sally
that's because I was part time

Caitlin
and you didn't know what you were doing

Beat.

it's too early to go to bed anyway. You aren't old, you
can't go to bed when it's still light

Sally
I have a headache

Caitlin
did you drink too much?

Sally
what? no

Caitlin
sorry I shouldn't have said that, it's up to you whether
you drink too much or not
you have a headache, it's your headache
do I get a right to even comment on it? No

Sally
Caitlin

Caitlin
what?

Sally
you know what.

Beat.

Caitlin
you can't get into trouble that I am here now can you?

Sally
I wasn't in trouble
you are allowed to have your students in your home

Caitlin
I was in your bathroom

Sally
they're allowed to use the toilet

Caitlin
I was in your bedroom

Sally
well if you were that was because you went in there,
I didn't say you could go into my bedroom. When did
you go into my bedroom?

Caitlin
I lay down in your cupboard

Sally
in my cupboard?

Caitlin
yes
I nicked a shirt

Sally
you didn't

Caitlin
I did

Sally

you nicked a shirt

Caitlin

maybe you should call the police
plus I've arrived with a dead bird and I'm obviously crazy

Sally

you didn't used to be crazy

Caitlin

I just killed a bird, things change

Beat.

Sally

what do you want?

Caitlin

I wanted to see you.

Beat.

Sally

please put down the bird, I can't have a conversation
with someone who's holding a dead bird

Caitlin

you always said new experiences are good, try talking to
me with the bird in my hand

Sally

why don't you just put it down?

Caitlin

I killed it

Sally

that doesn't mean you have to hold it for ever

Caitlin

how come you know the rules?

Sally comes and takes the bird off her.

Sally

in my house, killing a bird does not mean that you have
to hold it for ever. Okay?

Caitlin

I killed my father.
what does that mean in your house?

Beat.

Sally

what?

Caitlin

he's dead too
obviously, I can't carry him around so

Sally

you didn't kill your father

Caitlin

I did

Sally

don't bullshit me

Caitlin

bullshit?
don't bullshit, you say

Sally

your father isn't dead

Caitlin

he is

Sally

I would have heard if your father was dead

Caitlin

how? – it just happened

Sally

it just happened?

Caitlin

yes today, this morning
six, seven hours ago

Sally

where is he?

Caitlin

he's fine, dead but fine. Well apart from the fact he's a
cheating liar –

Sally

where is he?

Caitlin

in hell

Sally

Caitlin –

Caitlin

he's dead, what does it matter? Heaven hell he's dead he's
dead
I'll be dead someday too, what will it matter where
I am?
it's alright, you don't need to back away. I'm not going to
kill you.
and you don't need to phone anyone either.
it's all sorted.
after this I'm going to go and sit on that bridge by
Waverley. I have a bottle of Jack Daniel's, and two
bottles of cider which I think should pretty much do it,
and the trains are every few minutes – I was just coming
here to say goodbye when

Sally

you're scaring me.

Beat.

Caitlin comes and picks up the bird.

Caitlin

I think it's actually better if I keep holding it.
I'll be less scary to you if I am holding a bird.
because you can't do much one-handed. You can't hurt
someone one-handed, when I killed my father I'm pretty
sure I had both my hands free. You don't need to worry
about my dad by the way he was a bastard
I've just come to say goodbye
if you want to know
because if you were about to go and sit on the bridge
over Waverley I'd be pissed off that you didn't come and
say goodbye to me.
if I read about it after in the newspaper or something

Sally

that doesn't even make sense, you're raving
what are you even saying?

Caitlin

now or then?

Sally

both

Caitlin

I killed my father in the morning. This morning.
he was drunk so it was easy to do.
I didn't know what to do after. I went back to the house
I was just thinking about the fact that I have killed my
father, when a bird flies into the bedroom. In my parents'
house I should say. Their bedroom
I try to get the bird out of the bedroom because birds
shouldn't be in houses and it's not been an easy day, and
so I open the window and I try to shoo it out but the
fucking thing craps everywhere, like all over my recently
dead father's side of the bed and the book he has been
reading for years, so I kind of grab it – I didn't realise
that birds crapped so much by the way god that is not a
good design – so I sort of grabbed it to stop it crapping

as much as anything and then I kind of heard it make this horrible noise like it was in pain so I got the door thing, you know the stopper behind the door and I pulled it down on its head.
I still don't quite know where the blood came from though.

Sally

is that the truth?

Caitlin

I think that may have happened, yes.

Sally

what the fuck?

Caitlin

or something like that.
or maybe I did open the window and the sash broke and the window came down on its back. I think that is a more comforting series of events. The bird flew into the room and I was trying to get it out when the sash came down. Or maybe we could have I didn't kill my father. maybe that would be the best

Sally

and then you walked here?

Caitlin

and then I walked here.
I remember the noise though, the noise definitely happened. They both made a horrible noise. A sort of gurgling. So, it probably did happen.

Sally

where is your father?

Caitlin

in the garden.

Sally

oh god

Caitlin

no he isn't

he isn't in the garden I just said that to see if you would believe me

I didn't kill him in the garden. Why would you kill someone in the garden where the neighbours can see?

I killed him in his chair

Sally

you killed him in his chair?

Caitlin

could we say that I pushed him into the sea but it was okay because it was from this really lovely pier and we had just had a picnic and as he fell he sort of looked back at me and smiled?

Sally

I'm phoning your mother

Caitlin

you don't have her number

Sally

I'll find it on an old school list

Caitlin

because you were my teacher

Beat.

I didn't kill him

Sally

what?

Caitlin

I did kill him but I didn't kill him

he died because of me

we were going for one of those walks that you have to go on when you know someone has got something to tell you, and I knew it was one of those walks because my

74

mum wasn't coming – she's gone away for a few days
and there's been lots of shouting – and it's gone bad
between them, worse than bad it's gone rotten and he
said he wanted to take me to this place he used to go, to
talk and I said it was too hot and he said it didn't matter
he wanted to take me to a special place and we had to
drive for hours and he said he needed to talk to me and
he was drunk and he never drinks enough to get drunk
and I knew he shouldn't be driving and we got there and
walked and there was a stream like he said there was and
I kept waiting for whatever he needed to tell me to start,
and he just kept this silence and silence that went on and
on and eventually I couldn't stand the silence any longer,
the silence was making me sick and we were just crossing
this little bridge and I was just thinking I wonder what
would happen if he slipped and fell

Sally
    did you kill him or not?

Caitlin
    I don't know.
    I don't know if I killed the bird either
    they both seemed to somehow die on me.
    I think I must have killed my father because he was
walking one minute and the next minute he had hit his
head and his blood was washing away in the stream.
and I had just been standing there thinking I wonder
what it will look like if you slipped and died right now if
I didn't ever have to hear your voice say whatever it is
you have to say and convince me that you are sorry I
don't want to hear him being sorry and then he slipped
right then so even if I didn't kill him with my hand I am
guessing I killed him with my thoughts.
    also the fact that I nudged him

Sally
    you nudged him?

Caitlin

yes
or if I didn't, I definitely thought about it.

Sally goes to get something from a cupboard.

what are you doing?
Sally what are you doing?

Sally

I'm getting some wine, I need some more wine is that okay?

Caitlin

oh good I thought you might be getting a knife

Sally

why would I be getting a knife?

Caitlin

I don't know it just seems to have been a day of killing

Sally

do you want some wine?

Caitlin

no but could I open one of my bottles of cider?

Sally

yes

Caitlin

you're my teacher
you can't watch while I drink cider

Sally

you're nineteen now and not at the school
and, anyway, I think we are a bit beyond that.

Caitlin

okay that's good
we're beyond that, good.

Sally
will you put the bird down if I open your cider?

Caitlin
can I pick it up again after?

Sally
yes

Caitlin
okay.

Caitlin puts the bird down.

Sally opens the cider.

it's gone stiff.
look, it's all.

Sally
okay yuk

Caitlin
look at it

Sally
I don't want to

Caitlin
I can hold it by a foot

Sally
Caitlin.

Beat.

Caitlin
you sounded like my teacher then

Sally
this is what we're going to do, first thing is –

Caitlin
you sound like my teacher again

Sally

first thing is we're going to forget about the bird

Caitlin

please don't sound like my teacher

Beat.

Sally pours herself some wine.

Sally

we need to forget the bird, that's what I am saying.

Caitlin

I can't forget about the bird, look it's right here

Sally

the bird is an irrelevance

Caitlin

the bird is my punishment
I've become a killer

Sally

stop it

Caitlin

that's why I left the dog in the kitchen, no I said to the dog, if I come and get you I'll end up with a dead dog as well

Sally

the bird was bad luck

Caitlin

you think it was the sash?

Sally

do you think we should call your mother?

Caitlin

we did that thing remember in your class about how you can reframe any story?

Sally

I don't remember that

Caitlin

you can reframe a story by the point of view, or how you
tell it or what you leave in or out

Sally

oh okay

Caitlin

or sometimes even what you don't know at the time,
what you know later. That can change the story
maybe the bird just had a bad disease or something and
it just so happened that it died that moment

Sally

good

Caitlin

it's a trick though

Sally

I don't think you're a killer

Caitlin

but it's possible I killed my father.

Beat.

Sally

I'd like to know where he is, yes

Caitlin

I can't tell you

Sally

that he's okay

Caitlin

I can't tell you that either
he showed me on the map where we were going to walk
and how we had to get to this view, and all the time

I was thinking is this where he'll start and he'll tell me
about how he made all these mistakes but he carried on
walking just making me wait
more and more waiting –

Sally
I think you might be in shock

Caitlin
you sound like my teacher again

Sally
I'm just trying to look after you
maybe you need a biscuit or something

Caitlin
I think I might actually cry though I don't know why
I hated him, it doesn't make any sense. I hated him.

Beat.

Sally
when did this happen?

Caitlin
this morning
definitely.

Sally
do you know what time?

Caitlin
no but the sun came out just after.
and don't ask me how I can be sure of that when I can't
be sure of anything else.
I don't know the answer to that.

Sally
but you do know where he is?

Caitlin
as soon as I tell you where he is, it changes. It's not this
and biscuits. You'll need to go and make a phone call

and sort out all this stuff, and all the stuff will lead to an
answer, did I kill him or not. And I don't want to know
whether I killed him or not because I wanted to, and
either then I did which is bad although good in a way or
I didn't and he just slipped which is crap because if I
didn't then I didn't even do that.
if you want to kill someone isn't that as bad as actually
doing it? Or is it worse even because you don't even have
the guts?
I know he's dead.
it's okay you can make a phone call
I'll tell you my mum's number
though they're splitting up and he'd already moved out.
She might just tell you to fuck off and she is glad he's
gone.
go stick needles in your eyes I heard her say to him
go stick needles in your eyes right back he said.

Sally
who else could we call?

Caitlin
you don't want to hear how the last conversation
between my shitty parents went?

Sally
who else could we call?

Caitlin shrugs.

Caitlin
you?

Beat.

do you think it's going to be bad? Do you think I am
going to be punished?

Sally
it depends on whether you did anything.

Caitlin

do you believe in god?

Sally

of course not
whose blood is that on your shirt?

Caitlin

I think it's mine.
I think I hurt myself as I was trying to get the bird out. I
suppose they could put it in for some sort of analysis and
find out couldn't they? It's not my father's, my father
didn't bleed much and all the blood got washed away by
the stream. And I don't think it's the bird's and I am
pretty sure that I didn't kill anyone else today.

Beat.

but I agree there is a lot of blood.

Sally

do you want to borrow a shirt? Take that one off?

Caitlin

get rid of the evidence you mean?

Sally

I didn't mean that. I just mean, change into something
clean

Caitlin

you're being nice to me again.
you're being like a teacher when you are being nice to
me. I don't want to cry so please stop being nice to me

Sally stands up and gets a shirt.

Sally

here.

Caitlin

thanks. Is it yours?

Sally
does it matter, do you want it?

Caitlin
doesn't look like yours

Sally
it belongs to my partner.

Beat.

Caitlin
oh, your partner

Sally
Gee

Caitlin
Gee? Oh, Gee?

Sally
Gareth. His name is Gareth
he's away with work

Caitlin
do you remember once you said you owed me one?

Beat.

don't worry, I just mean maybe the shirt is what you owe
me

Sally
if you want the shirt –

Caitlin
I don't want his shirt, I am just asking if you remember
what you said

Sally
I don't remember

Caitlin
do you remember?

Sally

I don't

Caitlin

don't say you don't remember.

Sally

I don't remember

Caitlin

I don't want his shirt by the way, just by way of example
all the way over I was saying to myself, I hope she'll
remember
you said you owed me one and we both knew what it
meant

Sally

I don't know what it meant –

Caitlin

so you do remember?

Sally

I don't remember no

Caitlin

it meant a lie
it meant you owed me a lie

Sally

no

Caitlin

it did mean that yes.
you can't look after me or offer me your partner's shirt
and pretend you've forgotten that
it was after your class on *Hamlet*.

Beat.

Sally

Othello

Caitlin

Hamlet as well though. A bit *Hamlet* and a bit *Othello*

Sally

I never taught *Hamlet*

Caitlin

okay. *Hamlet* or *Othello*, it was how you retell it you said.
Retell the story where the good guys are the bad guys.

Sally

lots of teachers teach that way

Caitlin

I need a lie

Sally

I can't lie for you

Caitlin

why not, you won't tell the truth

Sally

what truth?

Caitlin

that you like me

Sally

I like you

Caitlin

that you love me, loved me then

Beat.

Sally

I don't love you

Caitlin

loved I said loved
before. Before you turned into this proper teacher.
and people that love each other help each other

Beat.

even if they only loved for a small moment sitting on a hill at the end of a Saturday when we shouldn't have met up but did anyway. Even if it was only then.

Beat.

Sally
Caitlin –

Caitlin
help me run away? I need to run away and I think you've got a car.

Beat.

I saved you. And you know I did without even being asked. I took all the flak, I said I was a stupid fifteen-year-old girl with a crush on my teacher. I said I was out of my mind, infatuated and I didn't know which way up I was, I said I wrote a whole load of stuff that didn't happen in that diary, I said anything.
because that is love

Sally
I don't love you

Caitlin
but you did.
and I know you did because whatever I might have said to save your skin, you kissed me first. Or if you didn't then you kissed me because you were determined to fuck me up even more than I already was and you knew that kissing someone younger who you're pretty sure thinks the sun shines out your bum is a good way to do it.

Beat.

Sally
what did you do to your father?

Caitlin

I don't know.
nudged him because I was angry but I didn't think he
would slip
he might have slipped anyway
or I might not have nudged him
I might have just wanted to
or I might have been able to get him out of the water if I
was quick enough and I might have just stood there
or I might have gone to him and tried to move him but
he was too heavy.
or maybe while he was drowning I just stood there or
maybe I wondered what it would be like to hold his head
there because I couldn't stand the spluttering that he was
making. Or maybe he started spluttering and I knew he
had hit his head and might end up damaged and I didn't
want to have to see my father live like a vegetable even if
he is a cheating bastard so I put my boot on the side of
his face to speed it up and it was for mercy really that I
killed him.

Beat.

you can say something if you want.

Sally

I don't know what to say.

Caitlin

say anything Ms Granger please.

Beat.

this is where you say yes
I'll get caught but we could just drive somewhere first
please just one night –

Beat.

I don't think you are a bad person, but you are fucking
this up so if you could say something. Soon.

Beat.

Sally drinks her whole glass of wine down.

Then she pours herself another one.

Beat.

I knew you'd know what this feels like.

Sally
what?

Caitlin
I haven't forgotten what you told me.

Beat.

Sally
I don't know what you are talking about –

Caitlin
you do know what I am talking about.

Sally
I want you to go now

Caitlin
of course you do

Sally
please leave

Caitlin
why? We both have secrets that's all. It's okay, you can
say yours was bollocks too –

Sally
please leave
I really want you to go

Caitlin
I really know you do.

Beat.

Sally pours herself another glass of wine. She gulps at it.

is that why you need to kiss fifteen-year-old girls because
you feel so shit inside?

Sally

okay I loved you

Caitlin

too late

Sally

what do you want?

Caitlin

I want you to say we are the same. Only I'm a bit
different because I own up to it. I came in here and said,
I killed someone.
I don't lie about the things I've done.

Beat.

Sally

I was eleven, I was eleven. Eleven years old

Caitlin

a man went to prison

Sally

he said he'd done it. Who was I to argue?

Caitlin

you knew he hadn't

Sally

I didn't. They got his car and the tyre marks matched,
end of
I was eleven.
jesus Caitlin I was eleven. Have you seen an eleven-year-
old, they don't know up from down. It was an accident.
I don't know anything. Did I or did he? The man walked
right into the police station. It was an accident a freak

accident he said. I was a kid. Why shouldn't we believe
him?

Caitlin

because it wasn't him

Sally

who is to say?

Caitlin

you are.

Sally

fuck off.

Caitlin

why didn't you ever say? No one would have blamed
you –

Sally

yes they would because I was cycling too fast and I
should have stopped and seen if the toddler was okay
and I knew I should but I kept on going and I never said
a word even though there was all this stuff in the news
and it went on for days and yes it's fucking shit living
with all that and knowing you can't tell anyone, is that
what you want?

Caitlin goes and kisses her.

Caitlin

I don't know what I want.
but I know that made it better.

She kisses her again.

please can I stay here just one night?

TWO

Caitlin is in the kitchen in the morning.

Her mother is with her.

Luci

> what the hell are we supposed to make of this, Caitlin?
> what the hell are we supposed to think?

Caitlin shrugs.

> are you going to talk to me?

Caitlin

> are you going to stop shouting?

Luci

> I can't believe you would do that

Beat.

> I know you can be crazy but –

Caitlin

> it's not a big deal

Luci

> Caitlin, she rang my number early this morning.
> she could hardly speak
> she started all apologetic like there was this thing to say,
> like it had actually happened.

Caitlin

> cow

Luci

> who is this I said?

Caitlin

> she'll be able to hear you she is just through the door

Luci

> I don't care if she hears
> she said I'm sorry for your loss, I said who is this?

Caitlin

maybe she's mad

Luci

oh she is mad, she is the mad one?
what the hell is going on?

Caitlin shrugs.

Caitlin

he is dead
we are literally talking about a dead person

Luci

he's not though is he?
he came to collect some things this morning
I saw him

Caitlin

he is to me

Luci

okay

Caitlin

and you are too.
both of you.

Luci

fine

Caitlin

I could have said I killed either one of you.
I thought about it as I was walking over.
which one shall I say I killed? Mum with a pillow or Dad
in the stream.

Luci

I don't understand you

Caitlin

you are dead, Mum. Everything that you were is dead

Luci
how can you say that?

Caitlin looks at her.

Caitlin
can I stay with Dad?

Luci
what?

Caitlin
you two are splitting up, can I stay with Dad please?

Luci
we aren't splitting up

Caitlin
you are splitting up
it's obvious you are splitting up. Why would you stay
together you are both awful

Luci
alright but why would you go and live with him?
that doesn't make any sense
you said you'd killed him

Caitlin
he isn't you.
that's the reason.

Beat.

Luci
alright. go ahead.
if that's where you want to be. I'll tell him

Caitlin
so you are splitting up?

Luci
I don't know.

we might not actually you know
we might stay together just to fuck you off.

Caitlin
please don't

Luci
who would you go and live with then?

Caitlin
I'm nineteen I never have to see you again

Luci
that's true.

Beat.

I know this is tough –

Caitlin
it's not as tough as you think Mum, actually I'm fine
about it.

Luci
okay, okay – why her then? Why come here?

Caitlin
I don't know that

Luci
her of all people

Caitlin
because I don't know

Luci
her who you got into all that trouble with

Caitlin
I didn't get into trouble

Luci
you did get into trouble with, you had to leave school

Caitlin shrugs.

she mucked up everything for you

Caitlin
I don't know, then is that what you want to hear?
I don't know
stop asking me. I don't know.
she owed me one

Luci
so, it was all manipulation?

Caitlin
says you?!

Beat.

Luci
perhaps you should go and stay with your father

Caitlin
Dad is going blind

Luci
what?

Caitlin
something is wrong with his eyesight

Luci
why would you say that?

Caitlin
because it's true
you told him to put needles in his eyes and now he has to
put needles in his eyes

Luci
you're really one fucked-up kid you know

Caitlin
well if I am it's because you made me that way
he says you blew a hole in everything and the whole
world blew up

Luci

I don't actually know what to do with you

Caitlin

he says that's why birds keep falling from the sky

Luci

birds don't keep falling from the sky

Caitlin

there were two in our back garden.
and another on the street

Luci

will you listen to yourself?
birds die I don't know why there were two dead birds in
the garden –

Caitlin

I'll tell her he is alive if you want

Luci

I told her he is alive
I told her that on the phone, of course I told her

Caitlin

well there we are, problem solved
only he's dead

Luci

stop it
she was as confused as me
right before she told me what a fuckwit you are
she put the phone down and said she was going to go
and pour boiling water on your head.

Caitlin

you didn't ring the police?

Luci

I took it to be metaphorical.

Caitlin

there's no such thing as a metaphor anymore, Mum.
Open your eyes. Stop living in the past. I say this is red,
you say it's red – but someone on the street, they say it's
blue. And someone else says it's blue and it's blue. Or it's
on the news. Blue! Doesn't matter if it was red. It doesn't
matter. It's bullshit. You don't have to act a way to be
something. I can be what I want by saying it. You say I'm
a dog, I say I'm a cat. Things that happened didn't
happen anymore. It's easy. Forget it. The earth is not
round. The moon is made of cheese. The holocaust didn't
happen, the vaccine is a hoax

Luci

he's not dead

Caitlin

okay he is not dead.
my mistake. Does it matter?
he's alive again. Great. You can be alive too if you want.
so what?
I'm going to put flowers on your grave
whether I will or not, who cares?

Luci

I'm worried about you

Caitlin

now? now you are worried about me?

Beat.

Luci

do you want me to be dead? Really? Is that what you are
saying?

Caitlin

I don't want to be Caitlin anymore.
that's another thing.
I am not Caitlin

Dad's not dead. I'm not Caitlin
I never was Caitlin in fact.

Luci
who are you?

Caitlin
I don't know.
I just know I'm not Caitlin.

Beat.

Sally walks in.

Luci just looks at her.

Luci
I'll give you three minutes. I'll wait in the car.

Luci goes.

Caitlin
cow

Sally
I could say the same to you.

Caitlin
fucking cow

Beat.

Sally
did you even kill the bird?

Caitlin shrugs.

Caitlin
do you think I did?

Sally
I feel like you've attacked me
I feel assaulted.

Caitlin
that's how I felt.

Beat.

sorry though. It is crap.

Caitlin walks out.

Sally is left.

Sally goes to the wine bottle she pours a glass even though it is morning.

She sees the dead bird.

The dead bird is on the counter top.

She looks at it.

She gingerly picks it up. She throws it away.

She breathes out like she has been holding her breath.

THREE

Loud music playing.

Sally is a bit surprised by the music.

She puts her bag down, looks around.

Sally
Mum?

She shouts at bit louder.

Mum?

Sally turns the music off.

Her mother comes in.

Helen
oh!

She laughs.

Sally

were you dancing?

Helen

no

Sally

were you –

Helen

not really, it's too hot, not really
I had some news

Sally

oh?

Helen

that okay if I dance when I get good news?

Sally

what's the news?

Helen

nothing really, good news for me but . . .
an award

Sally

oh

Helen

I know

Sally

today?

Helen

yes, today. Well I will get it, they've told me I have got it.
I have to go to the do, collect it. Say something

Sally

congratulations

Helen

thanks

Sally

who from?

Helen

government, for my 'ten things' schools initiative
I have to go to Holyrood –

Sally

you have to go to Holyrood?

Helen

yep, reception with First Minister, Prince Charles I mean
not that that is something you should be happy about
but – yes.
I got a thing!

Beat.

Sally

like just you or?

Helen

just me, few colleagues but
it's an award for me, yes. Ten things.

Sally

wow

Helen

anyway I've got to be there at three so I was . . .

Sally

dancing

Helen

it's not every day, so –

Sally

is the ten things the going-vegan thing

Helen

well yes that was one of them –
Holyrood, the First Minister, come on dance

Sally

you've had a haircut
new dress as well

Helen

just trying something –

Sally

I like it.

Helen

really?

Sally

yes

Helen

are you drunk?

Sally

no, why do you say that?

Helen

funny time of day to appear that's all

Sally

midday

Helen

yes funny time for you.
I'm not going to have all that long so – you can talk to
me but I might have to do my make-up.

Sally looks out of the window.

Sally

do you know you've got dead birds in your yard?

Helen

what?

Sally

there

Helen

oh fuck, don't look at them. I'll move them later.

Beat.

it's the heat
this hot summer, the Gulf Stream
something has happened to their feeding pattern

Sally

I saw lots on the way over

Helen

you remember Richard? He'll get a paper out of it

Sally

aren't you worried?

Helen

yes

Beat.

of course
I'm always worried.
but it's what you do with the worry. You have to be
proactive.
that's why I got the award

Sally

what will Richard's paper say?

Helen

I don't know.
that it's a freak thing –

Sally

that it's scary.

Helen

it's not a typical summer.

that's what it will say.

and the creatures nearer the bottom of the food chain are more vulnerable.

I don't know actually. When he writes the paper, I'll tell you.

Sally

Mum, I –

Helen

don't. Just for a minute

I'm getting an award today

whatever you have come for, just let me take you in.

let me imagine you have just popped in to see me

Beat.

Sally

so Gareth has rung you –

Helen

don't blame him

Sally

he shouldn't have done that –

Helen

he said he was moving back to Aberdeen

Sally

it's not definite

Helen

it sounded definite

Sally

we haven't decided

Helen

sounds like he has, sounds like he's gone
got a new job

Sally

well that's him
hasty

Helen

he rang me six weeks ago, how is Sally I said, he said it's
over. Then I rang you. Then I rang you again

Sally

I'm not good with my phone

Helen

I left a message
how many messages did I leave – ?
come over I said, do you need to talk?

Sally

I didn't get it

Helen

I must have left thirty messages.

Beat.

how long do you want to stay for?

Sally

I don't know

Helen

I'll have to think about it

Sally

okay

Helen

sorry if that sounds –
it's not a done deal anymore, you're a grown-up now. It's
not a done deal that you can come back here anytime it
suits you, no.

I'm not saying no, I'm not saying yes, I'm saying maybe
not.

Sally

okay

Helen

just this time

Sally

okay

Helen

I thought Gareth was going to work out anyway
I think we all thought Gareth was
I think everyone was, Gareth, god, Gareth was nice
I thought you thought it was going to work out

Sally

I thought it might yes

Helen

I'm not sure if you can stay Sal, is that okay. I'm not sure
if it's right this time.
there is a lot going on for me, there is a lot of good stuff

Sally

what else did Gareth say?

Helen

he didn't say anything

Sally

yeah right

Helen

he didn't say anything

Sally

bastard

Helen

don't blame Gareth, this isn't on Gareth

Sally
what did he say?

Helen
nothing

Sally
not true

Helen
okay you know what he said
why ask me if you know what he said?

Sally
he was lying

Helen
okay
so he was lying

Sally
you know he was lying, that is Gareth's problem he
always lies

Helen
please don't say that –

Sally
it's not true

Helen
why did you have to say that?

Sally
why do you believe him and not me?

Helen
for fuck's sake

Sally
really, look at me

Helen
you see I can forgive you anything, most things, most –

Sally

you want to go to my flat, see there is nothing in there

Helen

I can smell it on you
I can see it on you

Sally

it's been a tough few weeks but

Helen

months

Sally

okay months
it's been a tough few months
I admit it's been –

Helen

how much?

Sally

Helen

how much?

Sally

Helen

don't do this, Sal

Sally

I'm not, I'm not

Helen

please stop doing this

Sally

what do you want me to do, make something up?
okay I thought about it and I nearly went that way,
alright yes I might have bought some but I came to my

senses and I thought no that is just a shitload of pain I
don't want to do that, and I read my books and

Helen
I don't believe you

Sally
you do want a story

Helen
last time –

Sally
fuck off about last time –

Helen
you only come here when it's out of control

Sally
fuck's sake

Helen
don't get angry –

Sally
you don't believe me

Helen
would you believe you?

Sally
I knew you would be like this, fuck's sake, fucking
Gareth –

Helen
what do you want? You want me to believe everything
just because you say it?

Sally
yes I want you to believe me because I am your daughter
I haven't even drunk anything today

Helen
oh today?

Sally

sorry I forgot how perfect you are, you know everything in your award-filled life –

Helen

Sally

Sally

You know what, forget it
I felt a bit low and I thought –

Helen

I'll pay for some help

Sally

I don't want help
I don't want your money, fuck off with all that

Helen

what do you want?

Sally

I want you
I want you
I want you to make it better
I want my mum

Beat.

Helen

fucking hell, Sally
fucking hell, you aren't three.

Sally

I just want my mum

Helen

you aren't even thirteen. This isn't just a blank slate – this isn't TV – oh she wants her mum, and here is her mum. chorus of people watching. Oh look, she wants her mum. Mum, she wants you. You don't get to do that, do you know what it costs me to try and be there for you? I can't do it anymore. How many times, go on, how many times

have you come home and said that, how many times have
I gone okay and dropped everything, and I mean
everything, paid for whatever, sunk myself to try and get
you out of the mire

Sally
I don't know

Helen
you are too much for me
even mothers can admit defeat sometimes.

Beat.

people ask me, I don't always tell them I have a daughter
– no I don't have children or even – yes sometimes I tell
them I have a son, and when they ask what he does I tell
them he has a good job in an art gallery and a wife who
does people's gardens and works as a chemist and they
come over with their small children at the weekends.

Sally
bullshit

Helen
well maybe I will say it next time.
or what, how about I say my daughter died a fucking
awful death but frankly I am better without her. Would
you prefer that?
that she died last year and I had her cremated, and it was
sad but not that sad because she was a pain in the arse
and a drain on me and she fucked everything up and I
am far far better now she is a pile of ashes that I put
around the roses.
I can lie

Sally
yes of course you can
you can lie to the public and primary kids about the ten
changes they can make to their life so everything will be
okay

Beat.

Helen
why would you say that?

Sally
I didn't mean to

Helen
why would you actually?

Sally
forget it

Helen
and you wonder why I have to think about having you to stay
well go on then, tell me what you think?

Sally
no

Helen
what, it's a waste of time, meaningless, what?

Sally
you're an intelligent woman

Helen
so are you

Sally
look out the window, Mum
it's forty-two degrees in Scotland today

Helen
it's called hope, Sally.

Sally
it's a bucketload of shit

Helen
it's called hope

Sally

you're telling all these little kids that if they go vegan,
and stop using paper and recycle their shoes –

Helen

what would you have me tell them?

Sally

listen I am not saying anything, you do what you do, I'll
do what I do

Helen

you want me to tell ten-year-olds that they're all fucked?

Sally

I'm not saying anything

Helen

you say that it's too late and then what happens?

Sally

nothing happens

Helen

Scotland is fifty-two degrees next year

Sally

what does Richard say?

Helen

you find a line. You tell people that it's bad but not so
bad they go into despair, it's bad enough to take seriously
but not so bad as to paralyse

Sally

what does Richard say?

Helen

why don't you ask Richard?

Sally

is he getting an award too?

Helen

you want to speak to Richard, you speak to Richard

Sally

we all know that no one is really going to do what is required so

Helen

if you were going to die tomorrow, would you want to know?

Sally

yes

Helen

really?

Sally

yes

Helen

someone with a bullet?

Sally

yes

Helen

why?

Sally

so I could get paralytic.

Helen

exactly, exactly my point

Sally

better use of time than looking up recipes for quinoa.

Beat.

Helen

I have to go and put my make-up on

I've got two hours until I have to be there.
thanks for pissing on everything

Sally
my pleasure

Helen
how did you get here, did you get a train?

Sally
I walked

Helen
I'll get you a ticket back

Sally
it's okay

Helen
don't do that

Sally
do what?

Helen
like this is my fault.
it's you that came in here and threw shit around

Sally
there is no fault

Helen
it wasn't me that started drinking at thirteen, it wasn't
me that lied and stole, that wouldn't take help, that kept
going back, it wasn't me that broke every bloody
promise I ever made.

Beat.

I'm sorry that you need somewhere to stay but it can't be
here

Sally

I don't know what I was expecting

Helen

well think about it next time and think about what you
ask from people

Sally

because you got everything right

Helen

I didn't say that

Sally

what about when I needed you?

Helen

I was there
When you were thirteen, I was there, seventeen, twenty-
one, twenty-two, all the times in rehab

Sally

what about when I was ten?

Helen

I was there when you were ten

Sally

no, you were in your room and weeping

Helen

my husband died

Sally

yes my dad, he was my dad
but I was still here
you were in there weeping and I was out here, and
having to cope with it on my own

Beat.

Helen

why wouldn't you just say you are drinking?
it would be easier if you just told me

Sally

because I'm ashamed, Mum. I'm ashamed.
like all the other things I'm ashamed of

Helen

how much?

Sally

too much.
not every day but most.

Beat.

I can't find my way back.

Beat.

it's okay, I don't think it's a good idea for you to put me
up either. If I am honest I was hoping you'd be out and I
could drink my way through your drinks cabinet.
congratulations on the award

Helen

don't push me away

Sally

you know it's true though
of course I would drink it
if not today then tomorrow

Beat.

Helen

I'll make up the spare bed, is that what you want?

Sally

no

Helen

I'll make it up

Sally

don't

Helen

just take the bed

Sally

I can't

Helen

alright, I want you to take the bed, is that what you want?

Sally

if you actually did

Helen

I do.

Beat.

I do

I do. Of course I do. Okay?

Sally

I'll disappoint you

Helen

probably

Sally

definitely. I'll certainly get pissed and pee on the floor

Helen

I'll pour the contents of the drinks cabinet down the sink

Sally

I'll still get pissed

Helen

when did it start again?

Sally

a week ago
actually, a month ago.
when Gareth left, I don't know – when was that?

Helen

six weeks ago he left

Sally

okay but I have been drinking for six months
seven months, ten
see? I'll just go.

Beat.

I was probably going to lift some money out of your
wallet as well
and I know you keep fifty in the kitchen drawer –

Helen

aren't you working?

Sally

I haven't been going in too much, no.

Beat.

I don't know really what is going on with the job. I hate
it anyway. I hate the kids and they hate me, and I fuck it
up

Helen

what happened?

Sally

nothing. Me happened. That's what it is
it doesn't have to be that anything happened for it to be
a car crash. I am a car crash. Gareth was right to look
after Gareth, why would he want a car crash?

Beat.

Helen
come here

Sally
I don't want a hug, fuck off Mum

Helen
no don't worry

Sally
don't touch me –

Helen
I wasn't going to.

Beat.

Helen goes and touches her arm.

Sally fights her then lets her touch her.

Sally
that's enough no more

Helen puts her arms around her daughter.

Sally pushes her away.

Helen tries again, she almost has to wrestle her.

Sally wrestles back.

They fight for a second.

Finally Helen wins, she wraps her arms around her daughter, like she might never let her go.

Sally relaxes, lets her.

Helen
you're going to make my make-up run.

Sally
I didn't know about the award. If I had known it was today –

Helen

I always want to see you

Sally

like this I mean

Helen

it's just seeing you isn't always good for me.

Beat.

let me show you this hat. You can tell me if it's awful
I know the hair is too young for me

Sally

I'll get the train back
this is your day

Helen

you don't need to

Sally

I've done some stupid things, some terrible things, pissed
some people off and I've spent almost everything I have
and now I keep seeing things I don't want to see and then
I need to drink to make it stop

Helen

what sort of things?

Sally shrugs.

Sally

I see things literally before they happen
I've been here before, this, I've already had it
and if someone says something I think, yeah I have heard
that before, and listening to the radio, just now

Beat.

Helen

I think you'll be fine

Sally

and if I'm not?
I saw a man crossing the street, he nearly got run over
and I thought, I knew that

Helen

it's déjà vu, it's common

Sally

my eyes are itchy
I don't think I can stand being me.

Helen

so, you have been here before, how does it end?

Sally

you go and get your award

Helen

and you?

Sally

I can't see me.
that's the worst of it, I'm literally a blank

Helen sits down. She takes her make-up off.

Helen

I'll ring them, say I won't go

Sally

don't be stupid

Helen

put the kettle on

Sally

Mum

Helen

you're right
the birds are a development. I admit. No one expected
this summer to be this bad. Everything about this

summer has changed the statistics. And yes the ten things
project with schools is like a silvery veil, a haze that
makes the government feel good, and everyone feel that
what is ahead is controllable.

Sally
you must go
maybe this is a good haze

Helen
not really.

Sally
get the fucking award. Might as well.
I promise I will stay and be really boring and watch a
film on my phone.
everything is going to hell in a handbucket you might as
well enjoy the day. Smile at the First Minister and flick
the canapés at Prince Charles

Helen
I don't know –

Sally
drink the champagne. They dreamt up the award they
know it's bullshit. We need bullshit, hooray. Bullshit is
good. Maybe no one is capable of knowing the truth
anyway?

Helen
that's exactly what I say to Richard

Sally
thank fuck for you then.
let's see this hat –

Helen
will you be here when I get back?

Sally
yes

I don't know.
yes.

She takes a deep breath.

probably.

FOUR

Helen and Christopher, meeting outside.

On a bench.

Helen
and I know it's ridiculous and I am not naïve, god sake
I am not naïve but, god I am not even that hopeful but –

Christopher
how long is she staying?

Helen
who can say?
with Sally it could be – who knows. I think she's going to
be okay
this time I mean – you know, she could be

Christopher
you had a haircut

Helen
yes, I did

Christopher
it's nice

Beat.

Helen
do you think she might be? She really wants to be
at some point there has to be –

Christopher
of course

Helen
you think?

Christopher
yes, I think
I think she'll be fine.

Beat.

Helen
fucking hot still, isn't it? And there is this smell now,
have you smelt it?

Christopher
no

Helen
can't you? Like roses going off.
like just before you put them in the bin.

Christopher smells.

Beat.

Christopher
I was hoping I might be able to stay too . . .?

Helen
what?

Christopher
just for a day or so

Helen
you?

Christopher
don't sound so surprised

Helen
at mine?

Christopher
yes, at yours

Helen
sorry I didn't mean –

Christopher
Luci and I, well she's saying that I should –

Helen
I can imagine.

Christopher
so you could say I am a bit down on my luck

Helen
you'll get back on your feet

Christopher
yes but I was sort of hoping – ?

Helen
oh
sorry.

Christopher
not even for a day or two?

Helen
I don't think so

Beat.

Christopher
oh

Helen
I just think – with the timing –

Christopher
really?

Helen
well just right now

Christopher
you're saying no?

Helen
I'm saying no

Beat.

Christopher
oh right
you sure?

Helen
yes

Christopher
it's okay

Helen
I know it's okay

Christopher
just a bit you know –

Helen
what?

Christopher
of a surprise

Helen
I can't have you there with Sally. Do you understand?

Christopher
I understand
I think

Helen
do you?

Christopher
not really

Helen
she's fragile, I told you

Christopher
and if you didn't have Sally?

127

Helen
would you really want to come and share a bathroom?

Christopher
of course

Helen
we've never done it though, I mean maybe the odd night
but

Christopher
isn't that what it is about?

Helen
after all this time?

Christopher
we're in love, aren't we?

Helen
are we?

Beat.

Christopher
aren't we?

Beat.

Helen
maybe

Christopher
I thought you were

Helen
I thought I was too

Christopher
so, you aren't?

Helen shrugs.

Helen
it's been so long we've been doing this, whatever this is,
I can't remember.

Christopher
this is ridiculous, what are you saying?

Helen
I'm not saying anything

Christopher
I thought you did love me?

Helen
I thought I did too.

Beat.

They sit in silence for a second.

Christopher
yes, I can smell it now.
that smell, you asked me about that smell.

Helen
you can?

Christopher
yes.

Beat.

Helen
can I ask you something else, and please give me a proper
answer

Christopher
okay

Helen
did you at least ask me first?

Christopher
what do you mean?

Helen
for a place to stay, did you come to me first?

Christopher
I'm not even going to answer that

Helen
I didn't mean, we just both know –

Helen shrugs.

Christopher
why did you say that?

Helen
I just meant –

Christopher
I can't believe you don't trust me, there is only you
you know that, I have told you that many times. If I have
to tell you that again. Why do you do this?

Helen
and your wife.
there is me and your wife.

Beat.

Christopher
you said it suited you

Helen
it did
it did
why wouldn't it? Sexual excitement maybe with none of
the boring bits. Who wouldn't like that

Christopher
so, what is your problem?

Helen

it's not real life I suppose

Christopher

so let's do real life
I want the boring bits, real life yes please

Helen

now?

Christopher

yes now

Helen

now you are short of other options?

Christopher

listen Helen, can't I at least stay for a week or so? That is
all I'm asking, it's a simple request. You know all this shit
that's going on with Ollie, and work, I need some space,
I need you actually.

Helen

no, you don't

Christopher

you know I need you, we talk through everything

Helen

of yours yes
we talk through your stuff a lot

Christopher

I can't get through a week without you

Helen

if you needed me and I needed you, we would have done
this years ago
we didn't

Christopher

because you said you didn't want to

Helen

because you didn't want to

Christopher

you never listen
I never said that

Helen

you didn't do anything about it though
you never made one move to change anything, and I
suppose after years it's sort of telling
and I have listened. By the way
don't accuse me of not having listened
I listened and listened
the conversation always boils down to what you should
do and the answer always boils down to what suits you
the most. Ollie is shafting you, he has been for years. You
know that really.

Christopher

you are the only person I ever loved

Helen laughs.

stop

And then she laughs some more.

please stop

Helen

we had an appetite for each other I admit –
a comforting doughnut stop. Saucy and gooey, but that
was it.
my daughter is very probably peeing on my carpet right
now even though she promised me she would stay sober,
or if she isn't today she will be tomorrow. And of course
it makes no sense for me to be worrying about her but –
I'm going now.

She kisses him on the cheek.

sort it out, Chris.

Christopher
and Sally?

Helen
I don't know, but thanks for asking

Christopher
you see that's the thing about you, you are such a fucking hypocrite

Helen
what?

Christopher
you know what I mean –

Helen
I don't know what you mean

Christopher
I mean, will you tell her?

Beat.

and don't say she has a lot going on right now, doesn't she deserve the same as the rest of us. Sort it out you said.
you know what I am talking about.

Helen
she isn't well, Chris

Christopher
she believes he is dead

Helen
better she believes that

Christopher
he is living in America, he just fucked off.

Helen
okay I'll tell her

Christopher
when?

Helen
in time

Christopher
she might have siblings

Helen
I'll tell her

Christopher
will you?

Helen
I don't know, look don't look at me and expect me to get it all right. You can't use me to make you feel better. My mess is my mess, but

Christopher
tell Sally

Helen
tell Luci

Beat.

bye Chris

Christopher
and that's it?

Helen
pretty much.

Helen has gone.

Christopher
    fuck you then.
    thank you very much.

He looks around.

He kicks at the bench.

    fuck.

FIVE

Christopher comes back to the bedroom from the start.

He sits down on the bed. Luci is in the bed, reading.

Silence.

Luci
    what?

He looks at her.

She looks at him over the top of her book.

He looks away.

She goes back to her book.

He takes a big breath in.

He screws up his face like he is in pain.

Then he sits for a second.

Christopher
    it wasn't just Helen, there were others.

Beat.

    lots of others.
    actually, lots of others.

Beat.

Luci
oh.

Christopher
Luci? are you listening?

Beat.

Luci
yes.

Luci puts her book down.

Beat.

it wasn't just another lump
it's in my bones

Christopher
oh shit

Luci
yep

Beat.

Christopher
sometimes I felt out of control, like I needed the
excitement

Beat.

like maybe I couldn't stop.
I couldn't stop. I knew I couldn't stop. And so it just
went on.

Beat.

Luci
the doctors think it might all be over by Christmas.

Beat.

Christopher
I thought I was in love with Helen. At first. I wouldn't
have left you if I didn't think it was love, but then even

Helen wasn't enough. And so there was Sam, and Sam
was great for a bit, then she wasn't anymore so there was
Elaine, or perhaps Karen first, then Elaine.

Beat.

Luci
I wanted to die just to punish you. I wanted you to find
me dead and feel bad as I felt. That was my first thought
when they told me how serious it was. Good, I thought,
Chris will feel like shit.

Beat.

and that feeling of shit will go on a long time. Hooray.

Beat.

Christopher
I never wanted a child
when you got pregnant I thought I would shrivel up

Luci
when I got pregnant I thought I would shrivel up

Beat.

Christopher
you bore me
sometimes
a lot of the time
Caitlin bores me
this life bores me

Luci
you bore me
always

Christopher
not true

Luci
often then
you've grown ugly as well.

Christopher
  really?

Luci
  yes, grey and puffy.

Christopher
  I find other people more appealing

Luci
  I fantasise about leaving

Christopher
  so do I

Luci
  all the time
  I fantasise all the time.

Beat.

Christopher
  I feel lonely

Beat.

Luci
  snap

Beat.

  and sometimes I have a thought and I think, I should tell
  Chris that. And then I think, why bother? What does it
  mean to tell him? He probably won't be listening anyway
  and even if he is, he won't get it.

Beat.

Christopher
  snap

Beat.

I'm frightened by the world. By my job. I can't cope with
my job anymore. I just think Ollie might as well stab me
in the back and he probably should

Beat.

Luci
I think I might start going to church

Christopher
really?

Luci
I might.
I'm frightened of everything, Chris. Frightened of dying
anyway, maybe being dead would be okay.

Beat.

Christopher
I don't believe you will die

Beat.

Luci
I will

Christopher
well I don't believe it.

Beat.

Christopher
I voted Conservative in 1992

Luci
you didn't?

Christopher
I did
and again in '97

Beat.

Luci
fucking hell.

Beat.

Christopher
what do you want?
I'll do whatever you want?

Luci
I dunno.
If I have only got until Christmas I suppose . . .
go back to the start?

Christopher
be twenty again?

Luci
nineteen
when we were actually friends.

Christopher
I don't know, could we even –

Luci
I don't think I have ever really let you see me without my
skin on.

Beat.

Christopher
no, nor me

Beat.

it's not a pretty sight.

She smiles.

Luci
I'm not a fool. I'm not taking you back.
fuck that, sorry, Chris.
but I'd like a conversation.